TEN GROWING CHURCHES

TEN GROWING CHURCHES

Edited by
Eddie Gibbs

MARC EUROPE
THE BRITISH CHURCH GROWTH ASSOCIATION

British Library Cataloguing in Publication Data

Ten growing churches.
  1. Church growth
  I. Gibbs, Eddie
  270   BV652.25

ISBN 0-9508396-5-5

MARC Europe is an integral part of World Vision, an international Christian humanitarian organisation. MARC's object is to assist Christian leaders with factual information, surveys, management skills, strategic planning and other tools for evangelism. We also publish and distribute related books on mission, church growth, management, spiritual maturity and other topics.

The British Church Growth Association is a coordinating body for those interested in the growth (spiritual, numerical, organic and incarnational) of the British church today. It comprises researchers, teachers, consultants and practitioners who share information, insights, experience and new thinking through regional and national activities, a regular journal, occasional publications and other resources, seminars and conferences. It is located at 59 Warrington Road, Harrow, Middlesex HA1 1SZ.

Contents

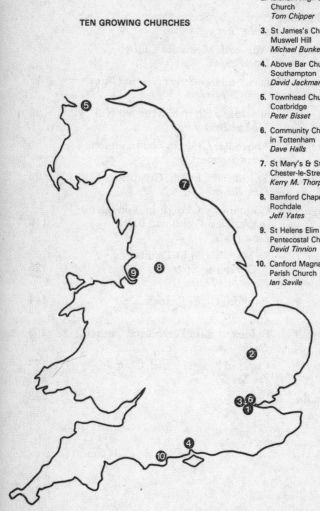

TEN GROWING CHURCHES

1. Walworth Methodist Church, South-East London
   Vic Watson

2. Isleham High Steet Baptist Church
   Tom Chipper

3. St James's Church, Muswell Hill
   Michael Bunker

4. Above Bar Church, Southampton
   David Jackman

5. Townhead Church, Coatbridge
   Peter Bisset

6. Community Church in Tottenham
   Dave Halls

7. St Mary's & St. Cuthbert's, Chester-le-Street
   Kerry M. Thorpe

8. Bamford Chapel, Rochdale
   Jeff Yates

9. St Helens Elim Pentecostal Church
   David Tinnion

10. Canford Magna Parish Church
    Ian Savile

Introduction

Behind the Scenes

Eddie Gibbs

Eddie Gibbs is an ordained Anglican minister who has served as a missionary in Chile and has been on the home staff of the South American Missionary Society. For the past seven years he has conducted a Church Growth ministry with Bible Society. Recently he has moved to Pasadena, California, as Assistant Professor of Church Growth in the School of World Mission at Fuller Theological Seminary. He is married to Renee, and they have four children.

When the Church as a whole has experienced unrelieved decline persisting over several decades, stories of full and flourishing churches may be more of a threat than a blessing. Such has been the case with the Church in the United Kingdom. Every major denomination has annual membership statistics which, if plotted on a graph, would present a ski-slope pattern.

However, over the past seven years there does seem to be a more hopeful trend. While membership continues to drop, attendance may now be on the increase. We have to say 'may be' because the statistics are not very precise, nor are they recorded by every denomination. Whether or not the data gives *evidence* of growth, there is now a more widespread belief in the *possibility* of growth. This improved morale is demonstrated in a number of ways, including attendance at Church Growth courses by thousands of local church leaders and a commitment to local evangelism as expressed in Mission England and other projects.

Not only are many more of the 51,000 churches in the United Kingdom contemplating the possibility of growth, but there is a growing pool of actual growth experience to draw from. A recent analysis of the data collected by the Nationwide Initiative in Evangelism of the churches in England indicates that eighteen per cent of the 39,269 congregations are increasing in numbers.[1] This means that there are about seven thousand churches with an encouraging story to tell! We can therefore learn from church growth experience as well as from church growth principles. Actual case studies provide models with which we can more readily identify.

With approximately seven thousand churches to choose from, how did we come up with the ten selected for this book?

They are in no way presented as the *top ten* growing churches. There are a number of well-known churches which are far larger than those described in the following pages. Although the 'league-leaders' provide great inspiration and may have some general principles of operation which can be transposed to a much smaller setting, they cannot serve as models as they are so atypical. With ninety-nine per cent of the churches in England and Wales having a regular attendance of under 300, we need modest situations with which we can more easily identify.

The fact that they are ten from among seven thousand possibles underlines the point that they are not freaky exceptions to be explained away. Each of them stands as a representative of the kind of things which God is doing through his people in many other similar circumstances. The stories recorded are not of the sensational headline-grabbing variety. They record developments and advances on a modest scale. If readers from other growing churches find that their own experience matches or even surpasses the events recorded, this will be a strength, not a weakness of this book. For at the present time the rate of growth is slow and stumbling. So, until the spiritual climate changes, it is modest models which are the most helpful.

Furthermore, in making the selection, we have tried to identify those churches which are mainly seeing growth through conversion rather than transfer. It is easier, if less

[1] *Prospects for the Eighties, Vol. 2.* (MARC Europe & Bible Society, 1983).

significant, to grow at someone else's expense. I have described this phenomenon as the 'recycling of the saints'. Yet churches which gain a reputation for spiritual vitality, and demonstrate a capacity to attract outsiders, will inevitably appeal to Christians on the move in search of a spiritual base which meets their own needs and those of their offspring, and to which they can invite friends with confidence.

The *Ten Growing Churches* represented here were selected either on the basis of knowledge of their recent history through attendance at Church Growth courses, or after consultation with church leaders who know the country and which of the churches within their denominations have a story to tell. All of the examples would fall into the broad category of 'evangelical'; in all other respects they represent a wide selection. Denominationally, three are Anglican, with one each from the Church of Scotland, Methodist, Baptist, United Reformed, Elim, Free Evangelical churches and the House Church movement. They are located in town centres, the inner city, suburbia, industrial towns, on housing estates and in the countryside. So they describe situations relevant to a wide readership. They demonstrate that church growth is not confined to the so called 'Bible Belt' areas and the roosting grounds of the migratory white-collar workers and their families.

I would like to express my appreciation to the ten church leaders who agreed to contribute. It is far from easy to write in such a detailed way about one's own situation. With typical British modesty most were resistant and needed some persuading, lest they should give the impression that they thought themselves a cut above their brethren who maybe were not seeing the same results. None of them is suggesting that others need only adopt his methods to experience a dramatic change in their performance. All of the contributors are as acutely aware of the still unresolved problems as they are of the modest gains. On looking back over the growth period they can see situations which could have been handled differently. They have all had the honesty and courage 'to tell it as it is', so that we can all learn from their mistakes as well as their successes. Each chapter, in addition to colouring in the background, presents a snapshot of how it is today. All the churches are in the process of 'becoming'; none would pretend to have 'arrived'.

This book provides an opportunity to learn from a range of experience. It helps to relate what is happening in our particular church to the wider scene. Many church members and ministers of necessity operate from a narrow base of experience. Many deacons, elders and Parochial Church Council members have only ever known two or three churches, and their ministers may not have experienced many more. So it is helpful to have a wider range of reference points.

Learning from the experience of others seldom provides short cuts to speed up progress in our 'patch'. Neither does it remove the toil and heartache. No chapter should be taken as a success-guaranteed model. There are no monthly check lists to be slavishly followed. The situations described here and the steps taken to deal with them may save the reader from some false moves, or may help to confirm him in a particular course of action already decided upon. *But there is no alternative to seeking the Lord's direction and resources for every situation.* Church growth is extremely complex, involving not only the make-up of the church membership, but also its history, the kind of situation in which it is placed, its distance from or involvement with the community, and background factors in the nation as a whole which may contribute to spiritual receptivity. Every reader's church is unique, despite the presence of similarities with one or more of the churches described in the following chapters.

Each author had freedom to write his contribution from his own perspective and style. In order to ensure a degree of overall cohesion, and to identify any common lessons which applied no matter what the situation, a brief was supplied. This has been included in an Appendix. By referring to this guideline the authors have commented on key factors in church growth so that general lessons can be drawn to help the editor compile his introductory chapter!

Having made a detailed comparison of the ten contributions there are a number of significant lessons which have come to light. These cover the broad areas of leadership, planning, structures, evangelistic initiatives and pastoral provision. The remainder of this chapter will be devoted to a consideration of these vital ingredients for healthy and sustainable growth.

Leadership to meet the requirement of the situation

Anyone who has made a study of Church Growth or has been privileged to visit churches experiencing church growth will be aware that leadership plays a crucial role. Although I suspect the contributors to this volume would want to play down the significance of their own contributions, they are each in their own way acting as catalysts in the 'chemistry' which has produced change and purpose-directed energy.

In acknowledging that, we do not wish to detract in any way from God's sovereign activity. But the Scriptures demonstrate and subsequent church history testifies to the fact that the Lord works through people. Or, to state the point theologically, he communicates incarnationally. In the model which Jesus both demonstrated himself and demanded from others, servanthood is the only valid leadership attitude. The servant is one who leads for the benefit of others, not to build up his own prestige. So the Lord warned the proud, pompous and power-grasping leaders of his day: 'You should not be called "leader", because your one and only leader is the Messiah. The greatest among you must be your servant. Whoever makes himself great will be humbled, and whoever humbles himself will be made great' (Matt. 23:10–12). Any leader who tries to play God is living perilously.

As one reads the accounts in the following chapters, there is no hint of a super-star leadership phenomenon. Each is gifted in his own way, and, while not denying those gifts, none would claim to be anyone out of the ordinary. In other words they are not the kind of people whose very presence would make exciting things happen, no matter how impossible the situation. I very much doubt whether such people exist anyway.

Knowing many of the contributors personally, I can vouch for the fact that they are very different personalities, with contrasting leadership styles. So there is no need for any church leader to feel that he has to undergo a drastic personality change to meet the requirements of a leadership ideal. Some leaders are 'up-front' extrovert types, while others quietly beaver away behind the scenes to achieve the equivalent results. If we know of only one church with a growth reputation, we may be tempted to compare ourselves with the leadership style of that church. We either say, 'If that's what church growth requires, then regrettably I clearly don't have what it takes,' or 'I'm not prepared to act in that kind of way.' The contrasting styles represented here deliver us from over-preoccupation with one model.

Having acknowledged the variety of personalities and approaches we move on to consider some common features present in growth-facilitating leadership.

The first of these is *vision* for the possibilities in the situation. Every person in a leadership position has people behind him who are either pushing or following him! The growth-enabling leader is inspired by a dream which provides him with the necessary direction and motivation to move a situation forward and to inspire those around him to want to travel that way. As progress is made and concrete evidence accumulates for all to see, people are reassured that the vision is neither a pipe-dream nor a delusion. Having begun to experience the benefits, they are more ready to 'own' the vision themselves and in the process their own horizons are extended. A true visionary helps others to open their eyes, lift up their heads, extend their focus and remove their blinkers. Even from the same vantage point, where you look determines what you see.

> Two men stood behind prison bars,
> One saw dust, while the other saw stars.

The second leadership quality which is clearly present is that of *commitment*. People like Charles Leggat at Coatbridge and Vic Watson at Walworth have invested their lives in the situation. In contrast, ministers who are either constantly looking over their shoulders for an alternative appointment, or who are sitting it out, seldom see solid results where they are at present. Such people are unlikely to perform any better when they move elsewhere, for the new situation seldom lives up to their expectations. As often as not the problem lies at least as much within themselves as in the situation which confronts them.

Those who follow want the assurance that their leader's heart is in the job: that he believes in what he is doing one hundred per cent. If they sense that such commitment is lacking, they are unlikely to accompany him into previously unexplored territory for fear of being abandoned once the going gets rough. Congregation members who are stuck in a situation, unable to move because of their family commitments, job security and home circumstances, know that their minister can move out with relative ease. The denomination has 'branches' throughout the country, and in most instances there is a house provided. Understandably therefore the congregation want some assurance that their leader is prepared to stay long enough to see through the outcome and repercussions of his ideas. Some leaders resemble the pilot who, having got his aeroplane into difficulty, then announces to the passengers and crew that he is bailing out to get help as he is the only one equipped with a parachute!

Church growth studies elsewhere have demonstrated that a growth programme takes between four to six years to consolidate. So the leader must be prepared to give an undertaking to remain for a reasonable period of time.

The third characteristic of growth-enabling leadership is being *prepared to take risks*. It is more hazardous to be on the move than to stand still. Sometimes, as at Chester-le-Street, the situation may initially get worse before the benefits begin to emerge. We tackle more confidently those situations with which we are familiar. It is far more nerve-racking to be innovative. The person who sees sustained progress strikes the right balance between over-caution and recklessness. The former stance restricts progress, causing people to feel it requires too much effort to get the leader moving, while the latter causes people to draw back because they do not trust their leader's judgement. Valid risk-taking entails counting the cost and weighing up the alternatives. If ever we were in a tight spot there are some people we would rather be alongside than others! The risk-taker has to establish a track record of achievement before people are prepared to follow. They want to know that he is a survivor and not a kamikaze pilot out on his one and only suicide mission!

In fourth place, a leader is one who *encourages the leadership potential in others*. In old English usage the verb 'prevent' meant to go before, hence the 1662 Prayer Book prayer, 'O Lord, prevent us in all our doings'. So often those who scramble to the front of the queue do so by holding other people back, and once they have assumed supremacy, they safeguard their position from all potential rivals by keeping them in their place. Thus the meaning of 'prevent' changed from 'going before' to 'putting obstacles in the way of others'. Such tactics are not what the New Testament understands by leadership.

The leaders who have contributed to this book give high priority to training others. They recognise and develop potential and have expansive programmes which provide opportunity for leadership initiative to be expressed. The leader is there to help others to grow.

As the church grows numerically and its ministries diversify, it is important that the minister or church leader *develops his own leadership skills*. On the whole, ministerial training is geared to equipping ordinands to be pastors of small churches, with little attention given to management insights, and church growth is such a recent phenomenon in the experience of many people in the ministry that it is hardly surprising if leaders of growing churches in the United Kingdom soon find themselves struggling to keep pace. Where does a British minister turn to learn how to lead and manage a church which has passed the 500-member mark? There are so few churches in that league that he is out on his own. His problems are further compounded by the fact that he cannot obtain the necessary resources to sustain the growth momentum beyond that point.

A cell group leader of 12 or less people operates at level one. A class leader, with a ceiling membership of 65, operates at level two, being one step removed from the primary group. A congregational level leader operates at level three with an upper limit of between 150 and 200 regular attenders at the most popular service. Beyond that level the task becomes more technical, requiring new management skills to ensure that the leader still has time to *lead* without becoming overwhelmed by the constant demands of the urgent. On this side of the Atlantic there is little in the way of training opportunities to help those who have reached this struggle-zone. At several points it is evident that the contributors feel the need for further training to increase their leadership skills.

The last point to highlight in our consideration of leadership skills to meet the requirements of the situation is to say that a church which has begun to develop promisingly *needs to be given space and support to encourage that growth.* When a plant is retained in too small a pot, its further growth is inhibited and it soon begins to wilt due to an inadequate root system and insufficient compost to provide nutrition and hold moisture.

A church likewise can become pot-bound. Resources essential to maintain its life-support system may be denied it by influential members resistant to the recent developments. While they may be able to frustrate progress for a time, they will eventually be bypassed as the economic power-base broadens through a growing membership which has been taught the responsibility and privilege of Christian stewardship. The problem is more intractable when resources are denied by church authorities above the congregational level. In some denominations staffing levels are controlled from outside and are more influenced by an allocation formula applied across the board than the actual requirement of any given ministry situation.

Churches which are continuing to grow significantly beyond the 500 mark need further experienced full-time staff appointments. They cannot get by on part-time helpers or by using trainees on short-term assignments. Such solutions merely increase the management problems of the church leader rather than lighten his load.

In making the point, we are not arguing that every church should grow into the super-church league. One alternative is for the growing church to establish satellite congregations or daughter churches. Another is for it to inject its life into moribund churches so that they too can begin to attract others into their membership. Whatever the best course of action, the options must be open for the momentum to be maintained. Space and support must be provided: otherwise frustration will set in and the church as a whole will be the poorer, as its shining stars begin to fade.

Plans and structures to effect change

Churches tend to be more concerned with process than
performance. They do not operate like commercial busi-
nesses, geared to achieve production targets and to market a
limited range of desirable products in the most cost-effective
way. Neither are they like military units with an authori-
tarian chain of command and the ability to exercise firm
discipline. On the contrary, the church accepts all-comers,
with a responsibility extending to include the weakest and
the youngest. It cannot weed out those who seem more of a
liability than an asset. Its primary focus being on people
rather than productivity, it cannot regard individuals as a
dispensable and replaceable means to achieve greater ends.
The ethics of the kingdom of God overturn conventional
values, emphasising that every individual is of intrinsic value
in God's eyes. The task of the church is to encourage and
assist people to discover their identity and self-worth, and to
find their place in the unfolding purposes of God.

A preoccupation with process to the exclusion of purpose
can also bring its own dangers. If a church which operates as
a business machine is in danger of becoming ruthless and
soulless, a church which operates as one big happy family is
likely to become trivial, introverted and eventually frag-
mented.

The churches represented in this book exist for a clear
purpose. In various ways they are all in the 'people growing'
business. They are approaching and attracting new people,
with a view to those people being changed by God. Such a
transformation, to be authentic, does not mean being
moulded by group pressure to produce a colourless con-
formity. On the contrary, it means being both challenged by
the life of Christ, as depicted in the gospel records and
incarnated in the Christian community, and also gradually
changed by the life of Christ operating through the life of the
believer. The objective is not to encourage the individual to
become more idiosyncratic, but to become more Christlike.
The goal of ministry, as stated by Paul, is for us to become
mature people, reaching to the very height of Christ's full
stature (Eph. 4:13).

In the light of this objective we must ask ourselves frankly whether there is evidence of changes for the better in the individuals who make up our fellowship and in our corporate life. The function of the church is not so much to provide a safe mooring as to prod people to keep moving – in the right direction!

The direction taken is determined by the goal to be eventually reached. As the goal of the church – which is to take Christ to all the world and to help all who respond to become more and more like Christ – will occupy us for our entire lifetime, we had better have those goals constantly before us. If not, we will end up disastrously off course.

As soon as we begin to define our goals more clearly, we find we have to make choices and establish priorities. This is the freedom and responsibility entrusted to us by the Holy Spirit whose freeing power releases us from the bondage of determinism on the one extreme and from the disorientation of aimlessness on the other.

Some church leaders and members are resistant to making plans and building structures to effect change, for fear of 'organising the Holy Spirit out of the work'. To the extent that they are objecting to a self-confident kind of planning which looks to God to provide a top-dressing of 'blessing' rather than a foundation of obedience, their objections are valid. But, as Richard Lovelace has cogently argued, the gift of the Spirit is to transform the faculty of our mind, not to replace it.

> To relinquish the guiding and superintending function of the intellect in our experience seems pious at first, but in the end this course dehumanises us by turning us into either dependent robots waiting to be programmed by the Spirit's guidance, or whimsical enthusiasts blown about by our hunches and emotions.[1]

In defining objectives and formulating plans, church leaders must both recognise their utter dependence upon the wisdom and resources of God, and shoulder their responsibilities in handling the freedom of operation entrusted to them by God. Living with this tension is a fact of life, and to be welcomed. Each provides a pull and

---

[1] Richard F. Lovelace, *Dynamics of Spiritual Life: an Evangelical Theology of Renewal*, Paternoster Press, 1979, p. 265.

counterpull to maintain equilibrium and contribute vital safeguards.

Objectives and plans are *forged in prayer*. This is emphasised in the case of Canford Magna Parish Church, St Helens Elim Pentecostal, and Isleham High Street Baptist Church, and is clearly implied in the remainder. The leaders are meeting regularly for extended periods of prayer, and continuing to lay their plans before the Lord to seek his guidance and to respond to his course corrections. In this way the plans are prevented from becoming paramount. They are merely one way, among any number of possible alternatives, to achieve an agreed goal. While goals need to be firmly grounded, plans can remain flexible. Prayer-based planning keeps those involved from becoming possessive and prideful.

Secondly, goals and plans need to be *expressed with clarity*. Ill-defined goals give rise to confused planning. Until you have decided where you want to go you are in danger of setting off in any direction, by whatever means, and enlisting what support you choose. Many churches give the appearance of a game of hide-and-seek, without the participants knowing precisely what they are supposed to be looking for, rather than a marathon in which all are going along an established course at their own speed, helped by those around them. Not so the growing churches recorded here. They each have their set of priorities which are clearly expressed and agreed upon by the membership core. Although there is considerable variation in the extent to which their priorities are formally expressed in a verbal statement, all seek to embody them in their lifestyles and in the emphases of their programmes. They recognise that their 'word of witness' may become blurred as much by inconsistency in application as by incoherence in expression.

As I write these words on a beautiful spring morning there is a grassy roadside bank nearby which proclaims the message, 'Spring is here'. If this were just a painted sign it might be open to challenge should the weather suddenly turn cold. But the words are formed out of daffodils which have burst forth to proclaim the message. It is a parable of what Christian communication should be: an impressive combination of proclamation and demonstration.

For a message to get across loud and clear it needs reinforcement by everyone making the message his own and sharing in the task of passing it on. In business jargon the goals must be 'owned' by the bulk of the church membership. It then becomes evident what the church stands for.

Thirdly, once goals have been stated and translated into concrete plans they need to be *implemented with initiative and conviction*. Plans must be given legs. In the following accounts one is frequently impressed by the depth of commitment of both church leaders and members. Here are people prepared to face the reality of the situation, believing that God is alongside, and that his presence is the determining factor. That realisation turns dreamers into prophets, for while the former get emotional, it is the latter who get involved. Where the Spirit of God is powerfully at work hearts are warmed, minds are set thinking, wills are stirred, and people move into purposeful activity. The church must demonstrate that it really means business if it is to establish its credibility.

Fourthly, *resources must be invested* commensurate with the importance and scale of the operation. Significant spiritual progress is not achieved by paying lip service to pious slogans or by making sporadic token gestures. It is the fruit of back-bending and not infrequently heart-breaking effort. Paul reveals part of the secret of the rapid growth of the church in Thessalonica when he writes, 'We always thank God for you all and always mention you in our prayers. For we remember before our God and Father how you put your faith into practice, how your love made you work so hard, and how your hope in our Lord Jesus Christ is firm' (1 Thess. 1:3).

The problem of inadequate resources has long been with us. When our Lord sent out the seventy-two workers into the Transjordan he warned them that the task would be beyond their capacity to handle (Luke 10:2). It has always been the lot of a few workers to face the challenge of gathering the large potential harvest. And remember Jesus spoke those words to the most religious nation on earth, where there was no shortage of housekeepers for God's house, compared to the dearth of harvesters to work in God's world.

Fifthly, the church requires *adequate decision-making and*

organisational structures to sustain its efforts and to conserve the results. Churches with a long sedentary history find this hard to grasp. Their maintenance-orientated and backward-looking committees are unable to cope with and to encourage growth and innovation. They frustrate rather than facilitate.

Churches able to sustain growth ensure that they have two kinds of structures: scaffold and skeleton. The *scaffold* is constructed in anticipation of the building which is to follow. It provides the framework on which the builders can work. The *skeleton* provides the internal strength to hold the body together and to enable it to move without falling apart. Since the church is always the 'becoming church', it will continually need to develop new scaffold structures in response to fresh needs arising either in the existing fellowship or in the surrounding community. In commanding the people of Israel to make the tent they lived in larger, God also reminded them of the need to lengthen the ropes and strengthen the pegs to support the increased spread of canvas (Isa. 54:2).

Sixthly, *progress must be evaluated honestly.* If the adopted plan subsequently proves not to be working, it must be exchanged for an alternative until one is found that is effective. We can become so accustomed to failure that so long as we are doing something, we do not dare stop to ask too many questions. An effective leader is ruthless in his evaluation. He is acutely aware of where he is and where he would like to be. He combines both realism and expectancy, in roughly equal amounts. A leader is one step ahead, a martyr is ten!

Initiatives to meet social, evangelistic and pastoral opportunities.

For people to take initiatives they require adequate motivation. Given the long history of numerical decline experienced by the majority of congregations in the United Kingdom, lack of motivation presents itself as a major obstacle to progress. Unfortunately the many programmes developed to meet social need in the name of Christ, or to mobilise congregations in evangelistic projects, usually overlook, or take for granted, the prior requirement of adequate motivation. As a consequence performance generally falls woefully behind expectations.

In reviewing the contributions to this volume I was particularly interested to detect how motivation was generated in these ten growing churches. There is a divine and human dimension to this dynamic. True spiritual motivation is supplied supernaturally by the Holy Spirit; it is not generated through human enthusiasm. Having said this, it is equally evident that the Spirit of God works through *people*, and often uses individuals to stir his people into concerned activity. In recognition of this truth, we devoted a section of this chapter to the issue of leadership. At this point, however, we want to place due emphasis on the spiritual aspects of motivation.

1. *Inspiring worship* lies at the heart of local church renewal. It is as we learn to 'magnify the Lord' that spiritual vitality bubbles up within the congregation and flows out into the community. We are worshippers first before we qualify as workers. Until this priority is established, our work is unlikely to point beyond ourselves to the Lord as its acknowledged source. In relation to evangelism, as Tom Chipper of Isleham Baptist Church writes, our purpose is 'not so much a beckoning in of folk but an uplifting of Jesus in each of our lives.'

The sense of the Lord's presence in Sunday worship, as well as on more informal occasions, has encouraged participation and released the creative potential of the worshippers as they have learned to open themselves to God and offer themselves to him in surrendered and sacrificial service. The variety of expression demonstrated by churches from a wide range of traditions is impressive. An Anglican church on the south coast, a United Reformed church and an Elim Pentecostal church in the north-west, a Baptist church in East Anglia, and a fellowship of community churches in North London within the house church movement, have all encouraged music groups in the 'folk' tradition, and visual impact through drama and visual aids. They communicate on all channels to reinforce the message. In the case of the Walworth Methodist church in East London a climate of trust has been built up which encourages people to share their hurts and needs, seeking the prayers and support of the worshipping fellowship.

Churches which have decentralised by forming several worshipping congregations come together in occasional combined acts of worship for mutual encouragement. Such times of inspiration also help prevent the smaller fellowships from getting into a rut, which can so easily happen when they stay in isolation. Celebration events provide occasions for innovation without threatening the regular worship pattern. If elements prove uplifting they can subsequently be introduced at local level with greater confidence. Conversely, gifts developed in the smaller, more informal setting can be shared with a wider constituency.

When churches endeavour to become more creative in their worship there is a danger of church services becoming a 'performance' rather than an act of worship. This results when those participating up-front are relying upon their own abilities and are drawing attention to themselves, and when the congregation is regarded by the 'performers', or considers itself to be, no more involved than the average theatre audience. Creative worship generated by a Spirit-filled community is of a different order. All, without exception, are participants, each contributing to the act of worship by offering back to God the gifts he has bestowed upon us. When properly used, these gifts point beyond those entrusted with them to the Giver, so that our awareness of his presence among his people is heightened and intensified. In our singing, for instance, we find ourselves no longer singing *about* God but singing *to* him. It is this immediacy of encounter experienced in song, prayer, preaching, etc., which provides the vital motivation for service. We are then more likely to want to invite relatives and friends and neighbours to share the experience. And, having once been, those invited may agree with the sentiment of the Jewish pilgrim of ancient times, who, on returning to Jerusalem for a great Temple festival, exclaimed, 'I was glad, when they said to me, "Let us go to the Lord's house" ' (Ps. 122:1).

2. If inspiring worship generates motivation, it is the *small groups* of committed people which provide the opportunity for involvement. When this small group infra-structure is

lacking, the worship occasions are prone to become detached from the issues of daily life and the sentiments expressed to lack credibility as they seldom lead to commitment.

From the examples of church life provided in this book it is clear that small groups play a significant role. (St James's, Muswell Hill, has seen dramatic development in this area – see p. 75). They form the essential building blocks for substantial growth. More extensive church growth research bears out this point. The absence of such an infrastructure means that a church's growth may resemble a balloon more than a building – likely to shrivel at the first prick of uncertainty, frustration or criticism.

The small group provides a cell in which healthy organic life can develop. Each person is encouraged to participate in an affirming environment to discover his or her God-given potential and to increase a sense of self-worth. On the other hand, members are also helped to recognise their weakness and dependence on other members of the body. The group must also learn to express its needs to God and listen corporately through Bible study and meditative silence to become aware of God's concerns not only for the group members but for the wider community in which they could have influence.

3. The need to *meet felt needs* is not only a cardinal principle of communication, it is also basic to Christian ministry. We have only to study the gospels to see how our Lord made the needs of the crowds pressing upon him a high priority. Yet he did not let these incessant demands dictate his agenda. He set out with his priorities clearly established. On the morning after Jesus had healed many people in Capernaum, Simon Peter went in search of his Master, who had wandered into the fields to spend time alone with his heavenly Father. On finding him, Peter exclaimed, 'Everyone is looking for you.' To which Jesus answered, 'We must go on to the other villages round here. I have to *preach* in them also, because that is why I came' (Mark 1:37, 38).

Vic Watson has expressed his church's commitment to meeting felt needs in Walworth by his heading, 'Making connections'. The church is demonstrating the relevance of the gospel in relation to the burning issues facing the community in the inner city: racism, police/community relationships, citizenship rights for those of Commonwealth origin, and unemployment. There in South-East London the Methodist Church is an outpost of the Kingdom of God which, having grown within that context, is able to express true identity. And at the same time, because the growth was given by God, that church is a pointer to a God-given future, beginning to take effect here and now.

Moving out from East London to the meandering, sclerosis-afflicted artery of the North Circular Road, we find three churches within the house church tradition engaged in a ministry of divine healing. Further afield in the East Anglian countryside, Isleham Baptist Church has launched out into a similar ministry. In the far north of England, the Anglican church in Chester-le-Street has a much appreciated 'Night and Day Core Group' providing people who will sit at the bedside of the terminally ill so that those on whom they regularly depend can enjoy a few hours respite. Near the south coast the church at Canford Magna is involved in a counselling ministry, running mums and toddlers groups, and senior citizens' luncheon clubs. The most physically fit congregation (!) is likely to be Bamford Chapel, Rochdale, with its wide range of sporting activities.

Such activities are part of the everyday programme of many churches. But the essential difference is that these are not regarded merely as *social activities* but as *spiritual ministries*. Many church halls have become premises for hire to all and sundry who are looking for convenient locations which they can make a base for their programme. Most of these activities have no Christian foundation, with group organisers eager to make clear they have nothing to do with the church. Thus the very building can be infected with a spirit of apathy or antagonism. And the church, in its eagerness to gain extra income from hirings, finds it is excluded from its own premises – at the very times when it wants the space to develop new areas of ministry.

4. Most British churches operate on a 'come-to-us' philosophy. In contrast, here are churches which have undergone a profound revolution in their thinking, by transferring to a 'go-to-them' philosophy. Growing churches

are prepared to *meet people where they are.* This entails meeting people where they are both in terms of their attitude of mind and their physical location. Bamford Chapel and St Mary's, Chester-le-Street, spend time with people in their own homes who are wanting to make wedding or baptism arrangements. Rather than a stilted interview with the minister in his unnerving study surroundings, they are visited at home, often by lay people. They are confronted not by the professional representing a religious establishment, but by people like themselves who are enthusiastically committed to a fellowship. While some ministers, like Charles Leggat at Coatbridge, Scotland, succeed in penetrating the barrier of suspicion and/or embarrassment their position generates, many of us do not. If this is the case those of us who are ministers may find the job of wedding and baptism preparation can be done far more effectively by involving lay people.

In addition to meeting people in their own homes, some churches are engaging in conversation in working men's clubs, pubs and public parks. The St Helens Elim Church trains evangelistic teams working under the gifted evangelist in the church's leadership team.

Genuinely 'meeting people' involves being prepared to forge continuing relationships, thereby demonstrating to those we are seeking to win for Christ that we are concerned about them as individuals. True Christian ministry always acts out of respect for the other person. It is sensitive to their world view, needs, aspirations and mental and emotional hang-ups.

When people new to the Christian family are asked how they came to be there, over seventy-five per cent respond that they started coming when they were invited by a friend. This is particularly mentioned by the Elim church in St Helens, the north London house churches, and in the survey undertaken by Above Bar Church in Southampton. The most fruitful form of evangelism is through the network of contacts we already have; this is especially the case when a new Christian realises the opportunity such a network provides for sharing his new-found faith.

5. Having succeeded in coaxing people across the

threshold of our church door, the next vital step is to *provide a way in to the fellowship*, so that the newcomer soon begins to feel that he or she belongs. In Chester-le-Street they tackle this problem by running a Basic Christianity course in conjunction with the morning service. Recognising that the Sunday service geared for all the family can become a 'spectator sport', they invite people out to the group after the worship time.

In St Helens they operate a three-stage evangelistic project called the 'Three C's' (programme: Contact, Commitment and Continuation) leading into an all-age Christian education programme. Here is a church which has taken seriously the need for adult Christian education, a concern which is tragically lacking in the majority of European churches. The north London churches have adopted the idea common in American churches of a Fresh Faces booklet as a way for the congregation to get to know the newcomers in their midst. They then incorporate new people by a welcome buffet, followed by a Christian Foundation Course, and a course in membership responsibilities appropriately entitled, 'What am I letting myself in for?'! Bamford Chapel also runs newcomers' evenings followed up by home visits.

Most long-term church members fail to realise just how hard it is for a new person to join the church and come to feel that he really belongs and that his contribution is recognised and welcomed. Early incorporation is essential to maintain a growth momentum.

6. Another way to encourage church growth is to *plan new churches*. Here in the United Kingdom this strategy is a better option for most churches than accumulating people under one roof, due to lack of building and parking space, and a society which is less mobile than on the other side of the Atlantic. Furthermore, churches which identify with and feel a responsibility for a local community may exercise a deeper and more effective ministry within that community. On the other hand, I believe that we must not lose sight entirely of the value of the 1,000-member-plus churches in city-centre locations, able to give a high visibility to the gospel and provide a wide range of specialist ministries beyond the resources of the smaller congregation.

Four of the churches represented in this book have already embarked on a strategy of establishing satellite congregations with varying degrees of local autonomy. Isleham Baptist and the community churches of north London are establishing new churches in the different areas from which their congregations are drawn. St Helens Elim Church is considering a similar extension programme. Canford Magna is establishing new churches on the new housing estates. Another church straddling the Hertfordshire/Buckinghamshire border has adopted a more innovative approach, using a church bus for outreach ministries aptly named the 'Chariot of Fire'!

Churches which have taken the bold step of releasing some of their members to start new churches have had to face the cost of depleting resources at the centre. But God honours those congregations prepared to release their best to extend the kingdom. Although their presence may be missed for a time, the Lord will provide others to take their place, so that eventually we are the richer for our generosity.

7. Lastly, growing churches tend to have a *wide horizon* of operation. Their mission commitment is not confined to Jerusalem, but extends to the ends of the earth. A growing church is almost invariably a sending church, so it is fitting that the publishers should combine this volume highlighting *Ten Growing Churches* with a second entitled *Ten Sending Churches*.

I hope that you, the reader, will be both inspired and stimulated as you read of the struggles, joys and pains of growth in the following pages.

Chapter 1

Walworth Methodist Church

Vic Watson

Walworth Methodist Church is an unusual church in a racially mixed area of the inner city, which has a declining industrial base and high unemployment. It is a recent development, and had congregations averaging 150 in 1984. The church itself is multi-national in nature and has a fifty-four room hostel attached.

Born in Manchester in 1928, the Rev. Victor Watson was educated in that city and started his working life in the office of a shipping agent. He spent a number of years in the Navy, including a spell of two and a half years in Hong Kong. He became a candidate for the Methodist ministry in 1951 and completed his studies with an external B.D. from London University in 1954.

He spent two years in a rural circuit in North Yorkshire and then with his wife Gwenda went to the Republic of Panama, where their three children were born. From 1957 to 1965 he and his wife worked to establish a school in Panama, and also organised the building of an old people's home. In 1965 he received Panama's highest decoration, the Order of Vasco Nunez de Balboa, as well as the freedom of the City of Colon and the Master Key of the Panama Canal.

Since returning to England they have been involved in the inner city ministry and are much concerned about the injustices caused by racism in the life of the nation.

A glorious past

Walworth Methodist Church, just to the south of the

Elephant and Castle on Camberwell Road, has a distinguished history going back to the early nineteenth century. It was famous between the wars for the pioneer work among children and young people instituted by the late Rev. James ('Jimmy') Butterworth who began what was known (and still is to many) as 'the first clubland church'. There are literally hundreds of people all over the world who will testify that it was here that they were first given a chance to express themselves and to prepare themselves for a better future than otherwise would have been possible from the back streets of the old Walworth. Jimmy Butterworth, virtually single-handed, created a purpose-built 'clubland church' which included a theatre, gymnasium, study rooms, lounges, canteen, games rooms and a lovely chapel. Tragically, the premises were bombed during the early stages of the war, not long after they had been completed and opened. Out of the ashes, there arose another suite of premises and also a hostel accommodating fifty-four residents.

However, by this time, the character of the community had totally changed. Many of the supporters of the church and clubs had moved out of the area; children who had been evacuated did not return; much redevelopment was in progress; huge high-rise estates were being built on the ruins of the old Walworth 'village'. The consequence of all this was that when Rev. Butterworth died in 1977, there was literally nothing going on at all on these magnificent premises. There was no church membership; there were no church services; the hostel was half empty; and there were no regular clubs meeting.

New beginnings

In September 1977, Gwenda (my wife) and I and our three children came to make our home here and to exercise our ministry. It was a daunting prospect and we didn't know where even to begin. Should we deliver leaflets? What would we write on them? What was there to invite people to? Should we try to reactivate youth work in an area where there were already many other youth clubs? There were many heart-searching questions! How could we make the hostel 'live'? What about the enormous expense involved in simply keeping this huge suite of premises clean, in good repair and (hardest of all) warm in winter?

We began by holding a Sunday morning service in the chapel for ourselves. We felt that this would be where anything of lasting value would start. There were just the five of us – but that didn't matter; we were making a statement. The church was 'open for business' again!

The frontage of the premises faces on to Camberwell Road – a very busy arterial road. It was surrounded by a six-feet-high wall with spikes on the top, made of hard steel. There was nothing to indicate that it was a Methodist Church and everything about it seemed to say 'keep out', 'don't trespass'. During our first few weeks, we had the wall pulled down and lowered to knee height. We planted flowers on the part in front of the Church. We had illuminated signs put over the two entrances – 'METHODIST CHURCH', 'METHODIST HOSTEL' – and shortly after, miracles began to happen; wonderful people came into our lives.

Wonderful people

John and Esther Badu are from Ghana. Esther saw the sign 'Methodist Church' and came to enquire about the possibility of having their baby boy baptized. Gwenda almost dragged her into the house for joy! The baptism was arranged for 11 December 1977, but before that date, God brought several other people into our lives – some as a result of the sign, others on the invitation of Esther and John. Kitty and Henry Coombes are the only link with the old Clubland who still come to our church. They actually met here during their childhood. Although now senior citizens and retired, they started to attend our services and to provide that link with the past which we all need. Kitty is now a Class Leader and Henry one of our Church Stewards. Then, Barry and Jennifer Taylor and their two children Michele and Paul came – they too had seen the sign and were looking for a church near their home. Wonder of wonders – Barry is an organist and Jennifer absolutely committed to giving her talents in service. Then David and Mary Rees came to take on the task of bringing new life to the Hostel. David is not only the Warden now, but also a Class Leader and Church Steward. Mary is our Secretary and 'mother' to our fifty-four hostel residents. David is blind, but you would scarcely believe that he cannot see. He is the son of a Methodist Minister who once worked in London. Looking back, I can only conclude that it was God himself who sent these good people to us. So it was that on 11 December, with all these good friends, and others who came, we had the lovely baptismal ceremony for Baffour Badu. John and Esther are still with us, as Class Leaders. Their last son Victor Yaw was baptized on 28 March 1982.

Participation in worship

As I write these pages, the membership of our church stands at 168 and our Sunday service at eleven a.m. is consistently very well attended, a fact which goes some way in destroying the myth that inner-city churches are almost by definition 'dead or dying'. There is nothing gimmicky about our worship. In fact we follow both the lectionary and the liturgy of our Church quite faithfully. We do however go to some trouble to encourage participation in the worship. Seven different people each Sunday have a part to play and their names are put on a rota which *everyone* has. It is their responsibility to read the Old Testament lesson and the Epistle for the day; to take up the offerings of the people; to welcome the congregation at the door; to give out the service books and the Bibles. At some point during the service, there is a 'walkabout' when people actually get up from their seats and move about to greet each other – especially those who are there for the first time. During the Response and the Intercessions, members are invited to share any good news or special concern. There is no Sunday School so that the children are not separated from their parents or from the rest of the church family. Nobody seems to mind if children wander about during the service – the preacher just talks a little louder! The services rarely finish before twelve-thirty, and more often end at one p.m.!

At present there are ten more people in a Preparation/Confirmation Class, preparing themselves for reception into full membership on Easter Day.

Growth – a gift of God!

Why is this church membership growing? What is the
explanation for a growth from 0 to 168 since that first
baptismal service in 1977? What is it that brings people
together Sunday by Sunday to what can only be described as
a fairly traditional church service? Most of our membership
is fairly young – there are only five senior citizens among
them. It is an ethnically mixed membership representing
some twenty-one different countries. I do not know what the
explanation is. I can only thank God for this vibrant and
responsive church family. To suggest an explanation might
be to suggest a 'model' for others to follow which would be
quite wrong, for there is no universal model for church
growth. Indeed, I can think of some areas of church life
where 'growth' might involve an actual reduction in church
membership!

Making connections

All I can do is to describe some of the things that have
evolved in the life of the church family which have come
about as a result of listening to and absorbing some of the
pains and sufferings which people share with the gathered
people on a Sunday morning. It is really about *making
connections*; about making the connection between the gospel
and the people where *they* are (and not where we may think
they ought to be); about responding to the call of Christ in
the levels of society where people live their daily life; about
making the connection between 'rescue the perishing' and
Mrs A's son who has had a hard time with the police, or Mrs
B who has been burgled three times, or Mr C who has been
made redundant, or young D who has suffered a more than
usual dose of racist abuse and oppression. Let me illustrate
this 'making connections' by describing some experiences
that have been shared (very often in worship) by members of
our church family, and the responses that have been made.

1. *Racism.* Aunt Liza came to this country in 1956. She
was told by her minister in Jamaica to make sure that she
found her way to her Methodist Church when she arrived in

London. She did just that. On the first Sunday that she was in London, she put on her best hat and went to the Methodist Church which her landlady had pointed out to her. When the minister came into the church to start the service, he looked down from the pulpit and saw Aunt Liza. He came down the aisle, escorted her to the church door and said, 'Your church is just down the road there.' She left with tears and never entered another church until she was brought by a niece to our church. She shared her experience in a Bible study group and then in her own stumbling way led us all in prayer, asking God to forgive the bitterness that had been in her heart all these years.

Racism isn't always as blatant as that! But whether blatant or covert, it is always painful to its victims. It can be seen in such attitudes as, 'We have no black people in our community so we have no problems.' It can be seen in the assumption that most white people make in identifying 'immigrants' with black people. (People from Ireland, Australia, Europe, New Zealand, are not really immigrants – they are white visitors!)

Joyce works at Guy's Hospital. She has a very responsible job and is in charge of a fairly large staff of cleaners. Recently Guy's Rag Week was held and in the magazine were printed the most disgusting racist jokes. They were scandalous to *any* sensitive person to read. Can you imagine how the many black people who work at Guy's felt when they saw these obscenities?

Our response when experiences like these were shared with us was to create two units designed to raise people's consciousness about (a) the all-pervasiveness of racism, (b) its totally anti-gospel nature and (c) the need to examine our structures (churches included) to deal with the racism in which we all – both individuals and institutions – are inevitably involved. Those two units are now in operation and are codirected by a white Anglican priest and a black Methodist lady local preacher. It is a brave new work which is already bringing a new perception, new insights, a deeper understanding and a heightened sensitivity. Not only do these units reach the leadership of the church; they also serve social workers, youth workers, community workers and many other groups of people who come into daily personal

contact with members of the public who perhaps never set
foot in a church. You may ask 'What is all that to do with the
church?' The answer, of course, is that it is the church
making connections with and responding to people where
they are.

2. *British citizenship.* Beryl and Sidney came to this country
in the 1950s at the invitation of the government to help in the
reconstruction of the economy. They came as citizens of 'the
United Kingom and Colonies', and had been brought up to
believe that England was the mother country. In 1962,
Jamaica became independent. Nobody told Beryl and
Sidney that they needed to do anything about that. As far as
they were concerned, they were British citizens – children of
the mother country. When the British Nationality Act was
brought into effect on 1 January 1983, Beryl and Sidney, in
common with thousands of others, were told in no uncertain
terms that they were no longer 'British', and that if they
wanted to take up their right to register as British, they must
pay £70 for the privilege of remaining just as they were in the
1950s! They had never been out of work and had paid their
taxes and rates like everyone else. How *unjust* that they
should now be faced with this extra 'tax'. There is a form to
fill in. Official forms are always threatening and often
difficult to understand, and you never quite know why
certain questions have to be asked about your private affairs.
    Our response as a church family to this new legislation was
to share the implications of it over a period of months during
church services. People would get up during the service to
ask questions and to express their sense of hurt and
bitterness. One of our members addressed the Synod of the
London South East District, and petitions calling for the
abolition of registration fees and expressing our sense of
outrage were signed. It was the wider church family making
connections – it was the gospel addressing people where they
actually are and being willing to share the pain.
    So far as our church family here is concerned, one of our
members, a young lawyer, still holds an Advice Point every
week to help people with the official form that has to be
completed and, as an expression of our solidarity as a family,
we have committed ourselves actually to pay the registration

fee for any who cannot afford it. Since then, the fee has been
reduced and I believe that that is in no small part owing to
people like ours who felt able to share their sense of hurt in
the context of the church's worship.

I do not know whether our membership has grown
because of this response. In fact that is not the point at all.
The point is that a connection is made between the gospel
and the people where *they* are and with what they suffer.

3. *Police and community relations.* The Brixton disturbances
in April 1981, among other things, brought into sharp focus
the poor state of relations between the police and the
community. It is not my purpose here to comment upon the
reasons for those poor relationships. Lord Scarman's report
has done this for us in great detail. I state simply that there
was a very strong feeling of 'Lord, protect my children from
the police' at large in our community. Something had to be
done! Printed below is a letter I wrote to the (then)
Commissioner of the Metropolitan Police, Sir David
McNee:

15th April, 1981

Open letter to: Sir David McNee,
Metropolitan Police Commissioner,
Scotland Yard,
LONDON.

Dear Sir David,
We prayed for you on Sunday, as we prayed for the
many of your men who were injured in Brixton over the
weekend, and the many others who suffered and are
suffering as a result of that desperate and tragic act of self-
destruction of a community.

I now write to you as a member of a group which has
tried unsuccessfully over the past twelve months to set up
a meeting between senior clergy and senior policemen in
London to discuss ways in which community co-operation
could be encouraged further in the difficult problems of
maintaining law and order in the London boroughs. At

our initial meeting with you in March 1980, we tried to express the depth of our concern for the peace and stability of the communities where most of us live. We came to share that concern with you and were enheartened by what we took to be your positive response in encouraging us further to explore the possibilities of mounting a one-day seminar.

We took note of the fact that you were in agreement that effective policing depends very largely upon a degree of trust and acceptance on the part of the public who charge you with your difficult task. We also took it that you too were concerned about the significant numbers in the black community who for one reason or another have grown to fear, resent and suspect the machinery of the law with regard to them. The very fact of your placing so much emphasis upon the work of your community Liaison Officers suggests that you acknowledge the depth of feeling in our communities.

I know that you will believe me when I say that none of us accepts violence as a solution to our problems. I *live* here; my church family is multi-national; my Hostel attached to the church has 55 residents from 22 different countries. The prospect of looting, burning and wanton destruction is frightening to us all. Yet over the past twelve months we have experienced St. Paul's, Bristol, the Deptford march, and now the tragic self-immolation of a community in Brixton, these two latter being quite close to us here in Walworth.

All of us have a lot of work to do. You constantly remind us that the Police 'cannot do it alone'; that you depend upon the members of the public for the effective policing of our communities. The pain for me is that a good deal of my ministry here in London has consisted in trying to foster good relations/understanding – only to find that months of work are brought to nothing after some insensitive (and sometimes brutal) incident involving young people connected with my church, and the Police.

I *still* wish with all my heart (as all of us do) to be in partnership with you in your work. We cannot do without each other. But *much* more needs to be done to bring us together; to share each other's concern for a just and peaceful society where people may live in mutual acceptance and human dignity. At present, I feel much trepidation and even fear. I think with sorrow of a fine young lady, a member of one of our churches, who has just embarked upon her training for the Police, for I *know* that to many of her black contemporaries, she will no longer be a part of the community in which she was brought up. She will, in their mind, have 'gone over to the enemy'. Such is the present feeling of many young black people in our community. In this time of high unemployment, this is perhaps best illustrated by the negligible response you have had from the black community to your recruiting campaign.

The meeting which we wished to set up was simply our way of trying to stand with you in your work, and an opportunity for you and your senior Officers of sharing some of *our* pain and frustration. No one expected that miracle cures would ensue, but perhaps we would have seen and related to each other in a different, less defensive context.

I write simply to ask whether the difficulties in setting up a one-day seminar between senior London clergy and yourself and senior Police Officers reflects an underlying lack of concern on your part, or perhaps an honest conviction that there is little we who actually live and work in the community can offer by way of experience and advice? At the present time, and from where I stand, I observe a deep division in our communities. Both you and I have been warned (St. Matthew 12 v. 25)! Can we not find ways, in mutual acceptance and trust, of working together for 'the healing of the nations'?

Yours faithfully

As a result of this letter, sessions were held on our premises over a period of five weeks, which brought together young police cadets and members of our church family as well as other leaders in the community. It provided a unique opportunity for members of the police and the community to listen to each other. There was anger, there was disagreement; but there was also laughter and shared meals and games. I have no way of evaluating the long-term effects of this effort to make connections, but for many of our people, it was the first time that they had experienced the established church actually trying to stand with them where *they* are between Sundays.

The efforts to maintain links with the police are continued in the church's involvement in the 'Help on Arrest' scheme which uses volunteers to go to police stations when juveniles are arrested and their parents are unobtainable. Volunteers from the church are 'accredited persons' and they go to make sure that juveniles' rights are observed. They are present when statements are being taken so that their stay in the police station is not prolonged. The church is also involved in a 'Victims of Crime Support' scheme which uses volunteers to advise, comfort and support those who are the victims of breaking-in, or mugging, or theft, or whatever. So we seek to maintain and foster a relationship with the police, the ambition of which is to gain mutual respect and acceptance. It is one area, I fear, which seems particularly difficult – perhaps even questionable, for I do not sense any noticeable improvement in police/community relationships.

Priorities

All these examples are merely descriptions of some of the activities that have evolved in the life of the church since 1977. They are not models to follow; they are responses that have come about as a result of listening and an effort on the part of the congregation to share; to hear the gospel in the context of real day-to-day experiences. This brings me to return to where we began; it is the heart of the matter – the gathered people of God for worship, praise and celebration. That is the foundation of our presence in this community. That is what gives people the motivation for all else that they do. It is the springboard on Sunday that enables us to 'plunge in' on Monday to Saturday.

Because this is such a vital ingredient in maintaining any continuity, we are also making connections with our two neighbouring Anglican parishes and expect shortly to be formally established as a Local Ecumenical Project. During

Lent, five groups met from the three congregations. On Palm Sunday we took to the streets in a united procession of witness which culminated in a united celebration of Holy Communion in the open air. It demonstrated where we are and was an open, public invitation to follow Jesus.

Starting with nothing as we did in 1977 has its advantages. For one thing, there are no traditions to fight ('We've never done that before!'). We were therefore not obliged to observe all the usual constitutional requirements of a normal church, with the customary large number of committees. We govern ourselves through four Church Meetings per year which are held quarterly on a Sunday after worship. *Everyone* is invited to take part, whether members or not. No one is excluded from decision-making. In addition to these meetings, there is a bi-monthly meeting of Class Leaders, Officers and Stewards which is for fellowship and sharing, and sometimes advises the full Church Meeting. It seems to work very well and does not test the loyalty of busy people in attending endless week-night committees.

Our Sunday service gives a central place to the reading of the Scriptures. In order to involve everyone in this, a Good News Bible is handed to each person on entering the church. Readers announce the page numbers and wait for everyone to find the place! This means of course that even if the reader's voice can hardly be heard, the people can still follow the lessons for the day.

We are greatly blessed by the make-up of our congregation. We are able to hear at first hand people from many of the countries that are in the news and on the television. In our Hostel there are people from lands such as Chile, Poland, Ghana, Eritrea, Ethiopia, Somalia, Iran and Iraq, Salvador – all seeking political asylum. There are students from many other countries. There are our own natives too! Together we seek to foster that mutual acceptance and yearning for Jesus' peace which can never be isolated from the demands of simple justice. Some of the Hostel residents attend our church services (including Muslims and Hindus). We are glad to affirm each other in the family of the human race – a family for which Christ died and rose again. There is an amazing mix in the congregation – young white, young black (employed and unemployed); professional people; ladies from a local hostel for homeless women; whole families of fathers, mothers and children; single-parent families – they are all represented and they all live locally.

It is exciting to be here because, apart from the Sunday service, you never know what will happen next! Some of the things that make the connections now will perhaps disappear – for example, the need for Registration for British Nationality will some day cease. Who knows what concern will be brought to us in the future? We only pray that the church family will continue to listen and respond.

Chapter 2

Isleham High Street Baptist Church

Tom Chipper

High Street Baptist Church serves a rural population in the area of Ely, Cambridgeshire, over a radius of about twenty miles. Although a farming community, it is also a dormitory area for those working in towns in the district. The church has grown from an average Sunday congregation of approximately 100 in 1975 to 350 in 1984.

Pastor Tom Chipper was trained as a structural steel draughtsman, and after two years' National Service was called to 'full-time' Christian ministry: he started studies at London Bible College in 1958. From 1961–65 he was minister of Maitland FIEC Church, Birkenhead and was called to Isleham in 1965.

He married Audrey in 1958 and they have three grown-up daughters. Pastor Chipper is a keen cyclist, and is interested in sport and classical music. He has led four tours to the Holy Land.

Isleham High Street Baptist Church is set in a rural community, which, in spite of an influx of population into small new housing estates, has remained stable over several generations, numbering about 1,800. It was registered in the Diocese of Ely on 25 September 1811, for worship by Protestant Dissenters, and was actually formed on 9 January, 1812, when three people, having previously been baptized, gave each other the right hand of fellowship.

The church soon grew, and its membership of 185 in 1910 was not matched until recently, with the membership now standing at 297. During its 172 years there have been twenty-one ministers, the present one being myself. I took up the ministry here in 1965, having pastored one church at Birkenhead for five years after leaving London Bible College at the age of twenty-six.

This village church, set on the edge of the Fens, has a good evangelical tradition and has been noted in the area for its hearty singing and adherence to the Word. Love of music has always played a part in the periodic times of spiritual uplift, during and following missions and campaigns. Unfortunately these times of blessing have been followed by years of decline, probably because many of the converts were swept into the church on a tide of emotionalism, rather than by a real Holy Spirit visitation.

Since the formation of the church, however, there has always been a core of those who longed for something more and whose vision led them to various forms of evangelical outreach. It is evident that the Lord had his hand upon the church, waiting for the time when willing and prepared hearts would be available to go forward in the way he directed.

Need for Holy Spirit power

Just over ten years ago my wife and I became increasingly aware that if the traditional negative Christianity was all that the church could offer to the world then its case was indeed hopeless. Disturbed by a lack of power in ourselves and the church, we were impelled by a sense of urgency to seek the Lord for his fullness, and in separate individual experiences received the baptism of the Holy Spirit. We know that only Holy Spirit power could have enabled us to witness to this experience from the pulpit, since we were sure, and, indeed, were proved right, that the majority of folk in the church, steeped in tradition as they were, would receive our testimony with a blank lack of comprehension.

Strangely enough, the first indication that there was some movement of the Holy Spirit came, not from within the church, but from without. Four older ladies of the village, who did not normally attend church, were pricked in their hearts, realising that they were lost and needed to be assured of eternal salvation. Without anyone urging them they came separately to our door, asking how they could be saved.

It seemed that the Lord was clearly saying he did not need to wait for a church to 'come alive' before he began to work. He only required that men should be found faithful, and willing to respond to every urge of the Spirit. No amount of striving on the part of man can bring about a renewal, although his co-operation with God is essential and imperative. In the realm of nature, plants grow and develop with no effort of their own; by just being firmly planted and allowing the sun and rain to work upon them, they move towards maturity. The seed sends forth a shoot, the shoot sprouts leaves, a stem appears bearing a bud, which blossoms forth into a beautiful flower.

So in God's creative work at High Street there has been an unfolding of his purposes, as we have been prepared to walk in obedience to him. As eyes were opened to a fresh understanding of the Scriptures, a few people began to see that the truths revealed there must be believed not only with the head but with the heart. John 14:12, which says, 'Verily, verily, I say unto you, He that believeth on me, the works that I do shall he do also; and greater works than these shall he do; because I go to my Father' (A.V.), became a reality and some dared to believe that the age of miracles was not past.

Healing

How wonderful the Lord is! Almost immediately he gave me the opportunity to put this belief to the test. For twelve years I had suffered from a twisted spine, which periodically put me out of action. Encouraged by my wife, Audrey, I stepped out in faith, and asked a fellow pastor to pray and lay on hands. I was dramatically healed. This confirmed in my mind what the Lord was able to do, so that when two ladies came to me with long-standing ailments I was able tentatively to suggest that the Lord could heal them. One was suffering from internal problems and the other from a neck injury, and both received healing after the laying on of hands and prayer.

By now our hearts were rejoicing, as we envisioned a New Testament Church, but it was not long before we began to feel frustrated, as so few seemed fully to understand the truths which we saw so clearly ourselves. True, there were a few folk who drew together around the Word, and others, who had previously been very wary, allowed themselves hesitantly to reach out and touch the reality of the Lord living in and through individual lives. Healing and deliverance – though not acclaimed as such – were used to show God's power at work and his desire to be operative in and through each individual believer. But there were only a few, and we so longed for the whole church to respond.

The Lord had to show us that he has his own way of bringing his purposes to pass. A prophecy was given, which initially we did not completely comprehend. It was based on Romans 11:7,8, and spoke of the Lord closing minds, eyes and ears, so that there should be lack of understanding. Before long we recognised this as a word of exhortation to stop striving to make folk understand, for the Lord promised that in due season he would bring in those who had not as yet heard, and as they embraced the whole truth of the gospel, those whose hearts and eyes had been closed to these truths would grow envious.

Conversions

The Lord was already putting his finger on the biology class of a local upper school. One seventeen-year-old girl witnessed to another student, who witnessed to his friend. He, in turn, witnessed to his friend, who drew his two brothers into the group. Soon they had added another four who spread the gospel until their biology master himself joined them. The whole group were led, one by one, to our church, where incidentally the biology master and his wife are now house group leaders.

This group of young people were eagerly seeking a new way of life. They began to meet together at our home on a Monday evening. Lovingly tutored and led by Audrey, they learnt the principle of living a life of complete surrender to the Lord, and handling the practical issues of life as true disciples. Their numbers grew from ten to forty in under a year, and provided the spearhead for much of the spiritual growth to come.

Motivated to give

So a church whose attendance averaged about seventy to eighty, and whose annual collections amounted in 1973 to £1,900, was gradually alerted to something new and wonderful. The emphasis was no longer on 'don'ts', but on positive, active Christian witness. We stressed that Jesus was not only our Saviour, but also the Lord of an individual's life. No longer was a comfortable, armchair Christianity possible; life was suddenly presented as exciting – and uncomfortably exposed to the attacks of the enemy, albeit as gloriously victorious.

After teaching on the Scriptural principle of tithing, and emphasising that offerings to the Lord should be made freely and cheerfully, we discarded collection bags and installed free-will offering boxes instead. It was recognised that the church body was responsible for its own support and should not expect visitors to contribute to church funds unless they clearly wished to do so. Every step of obedience we have made financially has brought blessing; collections increased dramatically to £5,000 in 1976, to £11,000 in 1978, to £52,000 in 1983.

It was an adventure to discover that giving always precedes receiving both in worship and finances. We come to the Lord initially to give to him, not only as we gather for worship, but in every aspect of our Christian living. He calls us to surrender everything to him, our money, our homes, our cars, our time, our talents. It has been amazing to see those whose attitude had previously been 'What's mine, is mine, and I'm keeping it', offering their cars, their furniture and even their homes to those who needed them. The Lord has promised that when our attitude to him is right that he will open the windows of heaven and pour us out a blessing (Mal. 3:10). He has surely done so over and over again.

Facing changes

The evidence of spiritual gifts began to draw a congregation from a wider area. People longing for a spirit-filled life, and dissatisfied with the lack of 'food' provided in their own churches, found at High Street a welcome and a sense of

God's presence. We discovered the truth of Acts 5:13,14, that, as the Lord moved in our midst, folk were irresistibly drawn in. The more we centred on him, the more folk came, and we felt that our evangelism became not so much a beckoning in of folk as an uplifting of Jesus in each one of our lives. While not encouraged to leave their own churches, visitors were accorded a welcome in the Lord which brought them back again. Each person was urged to pray and seek the Lord's will about their move. Others who came were back-slidden Christians longing for renewal, while personal witness brought in converts, who found that what they had been seeking was fulfilment in the Lord.

It soon became evident that seating was a problem, so we decided to carpet the floor and replace pews with chairs. The pulpit was also dismantled and replaced by a smaller one making room for extra rows of chairs. The large pipe organ was taken down and sold, and an electronic one installed. The seats in the gallery were padded to provide more comfortable seating. We built a small interview room in the upstairs schoolroom. Naturally there were those who were sad to see these changes – those who formed a core of village people to whom the church had been a lifelong institution and way of life.

More changes were to come, however. Whereas the service had been the traditional Baptist service with the Minister in sole charge, leading the prayers and choosing the hymns, a different pattern gradually developed. A short time of open prayer was introduced, which slowly grew into a time of praise and worship which has become an integral part of the service. We found value in singing *to* God rather than *about* him all the time, and folk were encouraged to recognise the difference and thus direct their thoughts aright. The former hour-long service has become extended for as long as the Lord leads, allowing space for spiritual gifts to be exercised. Speaking in tongues, interpretations, words of knowledge, prophecies and visions are all welcomed as the church joins in corporate worship. At the same time it is recognised that God is not a God of confusion, and that everything must be done decently and in order.

Most of the former core of members have accepted the changes which have taken place. These changes have never been superficially introduced by the leadership, but have all been as the Holy Spirit has directed; clear guidance has been sought over every move. As there has been a hungering and a thirsting for God the Holy Spirit has led and the church has followed. It is exciting to realise that we have not 'arrived': the Holy Spirit ever leads us on. He is still on the move and we wait expectantly to know the next step in our journey along the 'Way of Holiness' (Isa. 35:8) which leads to the Heavenly City.

New structures

We opened our home and the Manse soon became a centre where folk drew together; those with needs found help and encouragement among those who had found Jesus sufficient for every need. In this way we first experienced 'body life', although no secret meetings were ever held, for everything was announced with an open invitation (clarity of purpose automatically determined who actually came). As well as the Young People's Monday Night meeting there was open Sunday fellowship at our home. After the morning service many gathered with us for lunch and tea, and enjoyed a time of fellowship which knitted together those from the village with those who had travelled from a distance into the family, thus learning to care for one another and to share their lives. When numbers finally became so unwieldy that we could no longer cope with them, others opened their homes and gave hospitality to relieve the situation, and so another Scriptural principle was taught and learnt.

Later, such sharing was extended as men met together weekly for a 7.00 am Prayer Breakfast, and ladies gathered for a time together at the Manse at 9.15 am. This latter group has now increased numerically to over sixty ladies who meet in the church building on a Wednesday morning. Their time of prayer and sharing, under Audrey's direction, is recognised by the leadership to be a power house, as they bring different needs to the Lord, who has answered prayers in many remarkable ways.

In view of increasing numbers on a Sunday, a crèche for up to eighty small children has had to be provided, with Sunday School meeting for an hour before the morning

worship. The church caters for young people from the age of
ten up to twenty-one, both on Friday and Sunday evenings,
and on Sunday mornings in Bible Class.

Organisations such as Young Wives, which were not
aiming at spiritual growth, were disbanded after the Lord
had clearly indicated that they were no longer relevant. A
Boys' Brigade and a Girls' Brigade were formed in 1965,
when we first came to Isleham, as a means of contact
between chapel and village. They served this purpose
excellently, but in 1980 it was clearly felt that our youth
programme catered adequately for those over eleven, and
our desire for this age group was not to keep them at all costs
but rather to allow them room to form their own opinions
and come to their own understanding and appropriation of
the work of God in their lives. We now have 'Brigade' for the
junior age group only.

Clarity in aim is seen as important at all times and has
paid many dividends. This would apply to every service or
gathering from Sunday worship through house groups,
youth work and even the crèche, and we stress that, in
measure, each individual in the church should also adopt a
clear purpose for his life.

With church membership increased to 180 by 1979, it was
obvious that Audrey and I could not continue to be
responsible for all the visitation and care that were necessary.
With people coming from far afield for advice, for marriage
counselling, for healing and enquiries concerning Holy
Spirit baptism, the strain began to tell, and early in 1979 I
suffered a heart condition and was ordered to take a
complete rest.

House groups

Shortly before this the Diaconate had been studying the
housegroup system and its effect on family-type caring in the
church. It was now clear that with me out of action this
system should be quickly implemented. After seeking the
Lord's direction about leadership, seven housegroups were
formed.

Couples who already had hearts and homes open to God
and to other people were chosen to become housegroup

leaders. With the emphasis on 'family' there would inevitably be teaching involved, but primarily there would be care. For this the father and mother roles were seen to be of utmost importance. These housegroups were a cross section of the church membership, and were made up of varying ages, abilities and temperaments, so that each could learn to care for others and adjust to them as members of the Body who were necessary and useful.

At the outset members were given an option, and not all chose to join a housegroup; there were still some who found it difficult to adapt to change, and to the way new Christians were prepared to open up their lives to the rest of the Body! Eventually about a dozen left and joined other churches in the locality.

Christian basics course

As time has gone on, all those now wishing to join the church attend a thirteen-week Commitment Course, where they learn what the church stands for and what their responsibilities are to the Lord and his Body here on earth. There is an advantage in folk from no church and from other church backgrounds understanding what we believe and teach. The course covers such subjects as Victorious Living, Water Baptism, Spirit Baptism, Church Membership, Relationships, Relevance of the Word, Gifts of the Spirit, Giving, Guidance, Personal Communion with God and Holiness. In a congregation of three or four hundred people it is easy for folk to feel lonely and unimportant. This course provides them with thirty or so friends whom they quickly come to know really well. Relationships are formed which are continuing and blessed. Membership is still preceded by believers' baptism and all members are expected to join a housegroup. The number of housegroups has risen to fifteen, numbering between twelve and eighteen in a group, which meets weekly.

Evangelism – the outflow of life

The Lord has been gracious in restoring me to full health and strength. My responsibilities are now shared by two

other elders and by a team of men who are able to lead the
Sunday Praise and Worship times. Looking back, I am
convinced that the growth of the church and its impact on the
area has been brought about by the emphasis which under
God we have placed on personal holiness and utter
dependence on Jesus as Lord. Evangelism has to be the
outworking of a healthy spiritual life. Just as babies who are
given the right food and live in the right environment grow
to be healthy children, and develop into healthy, responsible
adults capable of producing healthy babies, so a church
giving out right teaching brings forth true disciples going on
in the Lord to make other disciples of the same calibre.

More than once the question was asked, 'When are we
going to begin an evangelistic outreach in the village?' The
reply given was that first we must establish our own
Christian values; then the outworking would of itself draw
enquirers, and attract those hungering and thirsting for the
living word and for something to fill the 'God-shaped void'
in their lives. That has happened in an inverted sort of way.
Those who came first were those contacted in the course of
work and school situations together with those who had
heard rumours about 'that church', and came to see what
was happening. Only over the past year or two have several
folk from the village begun to show an awareness and a
desire for the Lord.

Ministry to the whole person

With the formation of housegroups, and the teaching that we
are members one of another, the church has begun to be a
caring body. Everyone needs to be loved, and over and over
again we have seen the relevance of the song, 'I thank you,
Lord, that you don't want me to make it on my own.' The
church must care for the whole person, so a full-orbed
ministry is being taught. Personal caring and loving
outreach have touched and changed many lives.

One young woman, who had suffered from depression for
years, realised that while it was not wrong to seek medical
help, tablets were not the answer she needed. She came to
our home and begged Audrey to pray with her for the Lord's
help. She accepted him as her Saviour and Lord and the

Rock of her Salvation. She was finally released from dependence upon tablets, but still felt insecure. It was not sufficient to tell her that the Lord was her Rock, she had to know it for herself. When she finally realised this, life took on a new dimension and she was able to find her place in the church structure.

Another example was that of a young alcoholic mother of two, whose home was being broken up because of her addiction. She and her family were counselled and supported by a couple in the church, who allowed her to come to them whenever she was in a fit state to know she needed help. Much intercessory prayer was made on her behalf until the Lord broke in upon her and showed her what she was doing to her two beautiful children. She felt his cleansing power wash right through her delivering her and setting her completely free from her problem. She and her husband are now a living testimony to others who have benefited from their experience.

One young serviceman who had been heavily involved in drug pushing was witnessed to by another lad while he lay as a patient during a military exercise. The good news of salvation and forgiveness was eagerly accepted and he became a changed character.

Space will not permit me to tell of family relationships that have been restored, of the wife whose conversion gave her back her love for her husband, and enabled her to relinquish a good position to care for him when he became incapacitated, of those who after a life of deceit found Jesus to be the Way, the Truth and the Life. Satan's power over those who had dabbled with the occult was broken, and others who had thought that bell ringing or being in the choir gave them right standing in the eyes of the Lord, found a closer and vital relationship with him. People from all walks of life have found their needs met, but it is especially exciting to know that those in the professions, who might be expected to rationalise everything, have had their eyes opened to perceive that only a personal relationship with the Lord makes the incomprehensible acceptable. I Corinthians 1:23 says that, 'the preaching of Christ crucified is to the Greeks foolishness.' Only those who know the Lord personally can make sense of the gospel as the Holy Spirit witnesses within them to bring light and understanding.

Using gifts and talents

Once folk have become part of the Body they are encouraged
to develop and use their spiritual gifts and talents. Some help
with the Sunday School and youth work, others find
fulfilment in playing musical instruments or helping with the
tape ministry. No one is held back because of their youth or
inexperience, but at the same time all are watched over and
nurtured by others around them, so that their growth may
continue in the right way. Those introducing new people
care for them until they become established. Disciples, not
converts, are made and disciples go on to make other
disciples.

Naturally there were other churches who watched what
was happening and grieved that High Street appeared to be
taking away their congregations. There were those pastors
who felt they had worked hard for many years with little
apparent result. Now they saw a church in which growth
seemed to come with very little effort, and which was
creating problems for those who depended on effort for
results in growth. Fellowship was still maintained with these
churches to some extent, as it was pointed out to them that
there was no campaign to draw away their congregations.
People came because they were dissatisfied with unanswered
questions and unresolved problems, and were finding what
they sought in a live, God-directed body. The church is the
Lord's and he will build it, but he insists that it has to be
done in his way – all he requires is our willing co-operation
and undivided loyalty.

His church – not mine

He brought this home to me in the very early days of his
Holy Spirit revelation. It was at the time when I was feeling
frustrated and fearful of preaching out the new teaching in a
largely unresponsive church. I was sitting in my study
pleading with him for help to reach hearts in *my* church. I
heard him say to me very clearly, 'Whose church?'

'My church, Lord,' I replied.

Again the voice came, 'Whose church?'

'All right, Lord, Your church,' I conceded.

Then he told me that in his church I was to speak out boldly whatever he told me to say, without hesitation, and without watering down. The responsibility was his, my responsibility was to obey. It was a humbling and soul-searching experience.

An obedient life

As the church seeks to live an obedient life God reveals areas where love and concern need to be shown. There is no social programme as such, but one of the elders has special responsibility for hospital visitation and general oversight of people's needs. The housegroup leaders form a team of men and women who care for their particular group, contacting them during the week and being available when queries arise. Under them, each individual member seeks to serve in the sphere around him. One former deacon transports elderly ladies to their weekly Women's Fellowship, and helps to keep their gardens tidy for them. Others willingly provide transport to housegroup and Sunday services for those without it. One lady voluntarily visits those in Old People's Homes, while some act as baby-sitters on housegroup nights.

There has always been a strict adherence to the Word of God, and an emphasis on personal holiness and personal responsibility to live a God-centred life. Perhaps the following examples will serve to show how the Lord was speaking to ordinary church members at this time.

A man who had moved to the village and began attending High Street told the church that, when he left home as a young man, he had been given advice by an older Christian friend. This dear man had told him, 'When you see a man carrying a pitcher of water, follow him.' 'In this church,' our friend confessed, 'I have found just that. Water is life-giving, and here the Word of Life is preached. Our pastor has that word from the Lord and I will follow.'

An older lady, who had previously resisted change, had a word from the Lord. While on holiday she had seen huge Douglas firs, hundreds of years old, being felled. She expressed dismay at their destruction but a forester told her that the time was right. 'If they had stayed,' he told her, 'they would have died on their feet.' All through the night those words kept coming back to her as the Lord showed her how this was paralleled in the church situation. A church which will not accept change and will not move forward dies on its feet as so many churches have done.

Another young man had reached the point where he knew the truth of the above. He knew he must either move on with the Lord or leave the church altogether. Someone shared in the Sunday morning worship time a picture they had received of a house being built. Lying close by was a brick, useless and by blocking growth spoiling the grass underneath it. He knew he was that brick and that he must be built into the church instead of lying useless and hindering others. So the Lord went on speaking, and hearts were stirred and attitudes changed and softened.

Support for the church overseas

In a wider sphere the attitude towards missions and missionaries has become much more responsible. Instead of just contributing to missionary societies and then feeling absolved from further responsibility, the church has accepted an increased involvement in the lives of the missionaries we support. Three people have been sent out by the church in 1983, one as a nurse to Uganda, and a married couple as houseparents to Nigeria. These are supported to the extent of fifty per cent of their salary by the church, whose present policy is to donate twenty-five per cent of its income to missionary work. Three pastors have been sent out to take charge of churches, and other churches have been financially subsidized. The Baptist Missionary Society and the Evangelical Union of South America are also supported by some members, while the Women's Fellowship pay for a child under Tear Fund.

Decision-making

In order to prevent confusion, when housegroups were formed the Diaconate was disbanded and housegroup leaders took their place. Two elders were appointed, one employed full-time as assistant Pastor and the other employed part-time. Elders are responsible for decision recommendations, which are brought to the housegroup leaders for confirmation and to the church for approval. This system works very well, and church meetings are no longer 'a meeting place for folk with other folk to differ, and make their stiff opinions stiffer', but have become a time of grace and of listening to the Lord.

The church body seems to have accepted this change which was tactfully and gradually introduced. Much of the opposition from traditionalists has been prevented by clear presentation of aims, and the accepted assurance that the leaders are seeking the face of the Lord in prayer and are desiring to be obedient to him.

Elders, like housegroup leaders, are recognised rather than appointed: men who by their spiritual life and walk in God draw the respect and trust of the people. We are all very different in age, temperament and gifts. Paul, in his twenties, with a young family, fulfils a clear prophetic role in the life of the church; whilst Don, in his thirties, with school-age children, has a truly pastoral heart. We have been amazed at the way in which the Lord has blended us together, although many times we can only move in unity by laying down our personal opinions and desires, hearing God and then stepping together into obedience. Plural leadership has given breadth and variety to the ministry as a whole, and as with every step forward has led to increased outreach and blessing as if the Lord prepares his church and then gathers more to her – truly he is the Master Builder.

Growth will of necessity bring all sorts of changes and with the increase in numbers, there has been an increase in paperwork. This resulted in our employing a secretary and providing her with a small office in our home.

Starting new churches

More important still was the conception of a plan to plant out churches. Since structural extensions on the church site were a difficult proposition, and large numbers were already coming from the Newmarket area, it was decided that the first venture should take place there.

How wonderful that when we are in God's will he provides. Accommodation was made available at a local school in Newmarket seven miles away, and in January 1984 a band of forty-six adults and twenty-eight children were set aside to form a fellowship under a full-time pastor, and a voluntary assistant. Both had previously served as housegroup leaders, until the pastor was directed by the Lord to lay down his secular employment to become a full-time worker. After two months this church was totally self-supporting and had grown by some twelve adults plus children.

This is only a beginning, and once this fellowship is established we are sure the Lord will show us where to establish other daughter churches in the villages and towns from which people have come. Once again it is necessary to emphasise that we have not reached any final goal. The Lord is still directing our thoughts to personal relationships with him, and the fact that we must never become complacent and 'neglect our salvation'. There are continually new vistas opening out before our eyes and new battles to be fought and won.

When individuals or a church seek to be God-pleasers rather than men-pleasers, there is always a cost. If the trumpet gives an uncertain sound then the people become confused and unsure as to their next course of action. We believe that the trumpet has been sounded clearly with a single doctrine preached from the pulpit concerning the ministry and work of the Holy Spirit in the life of the believer, so that the congregation have had definite teaching on which to base decisions.

At the outset this meant a careful choice of those who were allowed to preach from the pulpit. Some people were hurt and indignant, but grievances were dealt with honestly, forthrightly and diplomatically. There were times when my decisions and tactics were misunderstood, and this hurt me personally. Over the years, however, I believe it has become clear that my elders and I are men who stand firm on what we know are the orders of the King of Kings. As we meet to discuss issues and teaching we endeavour to submit to one another in humility, no one of us seeking to exert authority over the others or to take precedence.

Wider links

As people have come to us from further and further afield, even travelling from a distance of over fifty miles to join in our worship, we have found our sphere of service spreading. Audrey and I have been asked to meet with the leaders of churches over a wide area of East Anglia. I also join in an Anglian Fraternal of ministers from all denominations who have a desire to see their churches moving in accord with the Spirit-inspired direction.

Looking back from the present vantage point it is possible to see where mistakes have been made, and situations allowed to drift instead of being immediately resolved. Perhaps we could have seen hurts and queries more quickly. The easiest way to judge when a car is going to turn is to watch its wheels. With hindsight perhaps changes in direction could have been discerned earlier and backsliding might have been prevented. Continually the Lord is teaching us lessons as we work towards becoming his perfect Bride. The Lord has said, 'If my people, which are called by my name, shall humble themselves and pray, and seek my face, and turn from their wicked ways; then I will hear from Heaven and will forgive their sin, and will heal their land' (2 Chron. 7:14, A.V.).

God has told us that he is pleased with the structure we have built, for we have sought to build in accordance with his blueprint, but we must be careful to recognise that this is not a structure purely for us to dwell in, but one on which he desires to build, and we look to him for the continuing ministries and enlarging of his work. He requires us to be pliant and usable, for then he has promised to bless. We have received 'mercy drops', but as we come before him with worship, prayer and fasting, we look forward to 'showers of blessing', and a great outpouring of his Holy Spirit. We are assured that he has much more in store for us, if we ourselves are ready and willing to receive.

Chapter 3

St James's Church, Muswell Hill

Michael Bunker

St James's (Anglican) Church serves an urban area in London N10, a turn of the century development which is now an established residential sector with both private and council housing. There is a low percentage of ethnic minorities and the largest individual group is professional and managerial. In 1977 the church had 240 on an average Sunday: by 1984 this had swelled to 450.

The Rev. Michael Bunker, the minister, was brought up in Lincolnshire, leaving school at 15. He then obtained an HNC in engineering, and became a production engineer. He and his wife both became Christians after they had married and settled in Ealing, and he studied for the ministry at Oak Hill Theological College. His first curacy was at St. James's, Alperton, and his second at the parish church of St Helens, Lancashire: he became Vicar of St Matthew's in 1970. The church later amalgamated with St. James's.

He and his wife have a family of four boys, of whom two have now left home. He lists his main hobby as 'fly-fishing – when I get the chance!'

They say 'love is blind'. If so, then you'll need to read what I say with some caution. For I'm writing with a deep love for the church here, a community of people I've come to love and respect over the twelve years that I've spent in Muswell Hill. But I have long been conscious, in spite of any blind spots, of having a special vantage point, as Vicar, from which to see God at work. Nevertheless, what I write is from my viewpoint only. Others, with their particular vantage points, may see a different perspective; and what I perceive today may perhaps be seen differently in the future.

I can here only describe to you, in fairly general terms, the vista and panorama. This scene, however, is made up of individual and personal experiences of God's grace and goodness. It is because God has been active in our midst that there is any story to tell, any scene to describe – 'Praise be to the God and Father of our Lord Jesus Christ!' Before I share with you something of God's gracious activity in our church today, I must first take you back in time and indeed even to another place – St Matthew's!

Starting with St Matthew's

The first eight years of my time here in Muswell Hill were spent as Vicar of St Matthew's, which was once part of St James's parish, becoming separate in 1938 and then coming back to join with St James's during my ministry. The first few years there were hard for all of us. The parish had a number of problems. For a start, the parish hardly constituted a distinct community in itself. It consisted of various kinds of dwellings, but lacked a real centre. The main shopping area was in the centre of Muswell Hill and our parish only had about three shops and just one 'Request' bus stop!

In 1970 when I arrived in the parish, there was a small congregation made up mainly of older folk, with a few young families and a handful of single people. We set to work with enthusiasm and quickly made friends. But it was hard, slow and often discouraging. In those early days it was difficult to break the 'this is an elderly congregation; this is a dwindling congregation' atmosphere. Most Sundays we could expect about thirty people to come to worship in the morning and about half that number in the evening. I well remember that experience of seeing only about six elderly people in the evening, and that awful Sunday morning when apart from myself and the organist, there were only three people in the congregation: of those, one was a churchwarden and another was my wife!

Those were difficult days and they lasted for about two years or so. I tried desperately to minister to the needs of the congregation as well as to plan and provide worship that would be attractive and helpful to any visitors who might just become 'newcomers'. I obviously didn't do too well. One painful evening I had the thrill and excitement of seeing a stranger in the midst of our evening congregation; a man in his late forties at a guess. I tried to conduct the service with enthusiasm and vigour and after what was, I thought, a stirring sermon, I went up to greet him before he left us. I expressed my pleasure in having him with us and asked if he lived nearby. His reply chopped me into little pieces.

'I live in Wood Green,' he said, 'and I normally worship in Edgware. I thought I would try and find somewhere nearer, but I think I'll carry on going to Edgware!'

A lot has happened since those days, praise God. I'm thrilled and excited to be able to tell you the story of changed lives, a growing fellowship and ever widening horizons.

The parish of St Matthew's consisted of a rather isolated council estate, some blocks of flats and several roads of single-owner homes and a fairly sizeable number of houses that helped to make up what we called 'bed-sit land'. It must be admitted that in the whole eight years while I was the Vicar there, there was little impact made on the parish. We made numerous attempts at outreach but with little success, however you try to measure it.

Nevertheless, at the end of these eight years, there was a lively Christian community. It was not large, but it was enthusiastic, and included a few faithfuls who could look back upon many years at St Matthew's – some even remembering worshipping in the temporary church building and being present at the consecration of St Matthew's Church in the war year of 1940. The main body of the church fellowship, however, consisted of young adults, mainly Christian graduates seeking their fame and fortune in London, whom the Lord brought to us in a wonderful way. These, plus a few young married couples, made up the congregation. We had very few families, which made it difficult for us to bring up our four boys, and hardly any Christians in the thirty to fifty age bracket, our peer group. What we lacked in experience we made up for in enthusiasm. Happily many of these folk are still with us today and active too.

A ministry of Sunday lunches

One development that was to have more positive results than we could ever have guessed at the time, was the launch of our Sunday lunches. Two things helped to spawn the idea. One was John Stott's book, *One People*. I had long thought that any church that was trying to have a biblical lifestyle should major on fellowship. John Stott, with his typical clarity, showed me how this linked with Christian worship and Christian service. I became eager to do all I could to help build a God-centred, outward-looking Christian fellowship.

This coincided with the rapid rise in inflation in the mid-1970s, which resulted in my wife, Mary, having to go back to nursing to ease the family budget and help us to survive as a family and still remain active in the ministry. She worked part-time and one of her sessions at the hospital was on a Saturday morning. With four young, active boys at home, I couldn't easily go out on pastoral visits. Hope of quiet study was wishful thinking! So I used these Saturday mornings to do what I could to prepare Sunday's lunch, thus hoping to take some pressure off my wife. I used to be a Work Study Engineer. This background reared up in my thinking: 'Why can't I prepare lunch for some of the church family while I'm preparing it for my own family?'

So this is what I did virtually single-handed for two years – how, I am not sure on reflection! It was a very rewarding exercise, though not financially, for although we made a charge, we aimed only to meet costs. The rewards came in other directions. The fellowship really deepened, moving away from the casual and superficial, which marks most of what we call 'fellowship', and is the inevitable result of our being with each other for such short periods of time. We met together for 'our eleven a.m. service and then afterwards for lunch in the Vicarage, until about three p.m., virtually every Sunday. We started to think of ourselves as a family! We always considered our endeavours in the 'backwaters' of Muswell Hill as a quiet little effort, but our Sunday lunches led to some 'fame' for a while. They were

even featured on the BBC's 'Women's Hour' and in the
national press!

Before I move on, it must be said what a vital role my wife
played during this period of our ministry. She ran the home,
played the major part in bringing up our four boys,
supported my ministry in many ways, including helping to
make ends meet with her part-time job – and on top of that
helped to entertain from thirty to sixty people for lunch
virtually every Sunday for two years. But perhaps few people
realised that not long after David, our fourth child, was born
in February 1971, and prior to going back into nursing in
1976, she had been ill! Proverbs 31 describes a very active
and industrious wife. We are told that her husband 'praises
her' (v.28). Let me do the same. This raises the thought in
my mind, 'What church can grow that doesn't have the
commitment and support of the pastor's wife?'

What did the future hold?

During the early part of 1977 I did, however, begin to
question just what God wanted for us in the future. The
church buildings were in need of major repairs and
improvement. Although we had ourselves reordered our
church interior, installed our own central heating system,
rewired, replumbed and reordered our church hall, I was
still very uneasy about asking our people to invest much
more time, energy and financial resources in this work as it
was. I thought, studied, prayed and then shared my thoughts
with a few of the young leaders of the church. (The average
age of our P.C.C. at this time was about 25!) One
memorable evening I shared with this inner core my feelings
that we were as a fellowship at a cross-roads. In substance,
my message to them was that although we now had a small
but lively fellowship, we needed to be aware of the following
points:

1. *Our fellowship wasn't a healthy mix.* It was made up of a few
elderly folk; a few young marrieds without children; a few
families with children. By far the greatest section, however,
was made up of young (under twenty-five) single men and

women. We had very few over the age of thirty and under sixty-five!

2. *We hadn't made any noticeable impact on our parish over the past seven years.* We had tried with varying degrees of imagination, effort and commitment, but with little, if any, measurable success. Looking through the records of the church it seemed to me that no previous generation in its history had had any noticeable impact either.

3. *The church plant was in very urgent need of attention.* We had made a number of temporary rearrangements. But, for our buildings to be brought up to modern standards for use by a contemporary church trying to meet the needs and demands of the local community, a great deal of money – many thousands of pounds – would have to be spent.

4. This led to the biggest question: *Was this church and ministry really a viable proposition on its own?* Was God telling us to think again?

This meeting went on long into the early hours of the morning. It was finally decided that I would draft a report to our Bishop. In typical fashion he quickly responded and a very warm and positive discussion took place between the two of us as we looked at the implications of what had been reported.

Joining with St James's

Just before Christmas 1977 the then Vicar of St James's, Bill Allam, sadly died. A few months later the Bishop asked me if I would go to St James's as Vicar and take the people of St Matthew's with me. The whole prospect of coming to this great church with its long tradition, right in the heart of the community and strategically set on the top of the hill, was so overwhelming I could hardly believe it. On Monday, 7 April 1978 I was Instituted. The day before was my last Sunday as Vicar of St Matthew's and was the last time the building was used as a place of public worship. The decision for the whole church to move in this way was carried unanimously at an open meeting of the St Matthew's congregation! It wasn't an easy decision for some of our members who had been there for many, many years. They had worked, saved and seen the church built as well as, some years afterwards, the Vicarage. It ws a bold act of courage and trust on their part. Since those days, I haven't once heard anyone express any regrets. On the contrary, expressions of the rightness of that decision are still being heard today.

It should also be said, at this point, that the people of St James's exercised similar courage and trust too! They had a choice. They didn't have to have the Vicar from down the road. These were difficult days for the people of St James's. There were a number of people within the congregation who could remember their younger days when the 700-seater church was full every Sunday morning! That was in the past. At the time of my move, the congregation was at a low ebb for a number of reasons – not least the sad loss of their much-loved and respected Vicar, who had been their faithful pastor for some ten years. His death was a bitter blow for a church finding it hard to come to terms with the changing face of the community, at the centre of which they stood. Sunday worship was conducted in cathedral-style. Although there was a very fine organ, by now the choir was small and the congregation was in decline.

I was in that very fortunate position of knowing what to expect. I had worshipped at St James's a number of times, and already knew a good many of the congregation and was in a position to begin to assess, with at least the possibility of some degree of accuracy, the present life of the church and its potential. Clearly something had to be done right at the beginning to lift expectations. How was that to happen? How were the necessary changes to be implemented to bring the two congregations together happily, and what was to be the time-scale of it all?

I had the wonderful fortune to have a close friend who lived in Muswell Hill, who was a committed Christian and a clear thinker to top that, and yet didn't worship at either St James's or St Matthew's. I was therefore able to share and talk through the many possible ways forward. It became obvious that I had to strike a new note right from the beginning.

Long before I had had any exposure to 'church growth' literature, other than the Bible of course, I felt that I needed to look to the Lord for help in a number of areas especially. A strong positive lead was crucial, particularly in the areas of worship, Bible exposition, fellowship and parish planning, right at the outset of this ministry.

My wife and I decided to do our best to keep on our Sunday lunches to help encourage and build up the fellowship. Although our Sunday work-load had more than doubled, and we still had to function from St Matthew's Vicarage while St James's Vicarage was being improved, we still felt these should continue. Although we hoped people would book in advance, we never knew how many to expect. We often had thirty people booked for lunch and sixty or seventy arrived! On one occasion we had ninety-five! By then, fortunately, we had a small team to help us.

Ever since my student days I've been a convinced, but struggling, expositor of the Word. Right from the beginning at St Matthew's, I had committed myself to serious, but I hope not dull, systematic, expository preaching. This I continued at St James's. I tried to keep a high standard of preparation in spite of all the other pressures. How well I succeeded I am not sure, but not many left and people started to come in greater numbers and were warm in their encouragement. I was excited to be able to preach the Word and people seemed to appreciate this Bible-centred ministry.

Worship : a most important area

Dealing with the worship was to be one of the most difficult and delicate areas for attention, and yet perhaps the most important. Before God, I felt I had to do all that was within my reach, to provide services of worship that were truly God-centred and honouring to him as well as providing an enriching experience for the congregation. Without going into details, it was necessary to appoint a new organist and establish a different tradition in congregational music. This we hoped to do while building upon the high standards that had been upheld.

The problem of two congregations coming together for worship had to be faced – they had quite different traditions. Both couldn't have it all their own way! So both had to be prepared for changes. They responded to the challenge with remarkable generosity. After some of the leaders from both churches had discussed a proposal for a new pattern for Sunday worship, a final plan was presented as the way forward in this area. This basic monthly plan, which has hardly changed since then, was as follows:

8.00 a.m.   Holy Communion (Every Sunday)
            Originally we planned to use the Prayer Book and Series 3 liturgies alternately, but we soon realised that the sort of people who came to this service appreciated the Prayer Book service, and so now use that solely.

11.00 a.m. 1st Sunday – Morning Prayer – Prayer Book
            2nd Sunday – Morning Prayer – Series 3
            3rd Sunday – Holy Communion – Series 3
            4th Sunday – Family Service – Using some Series 3 sections.

6.30 p.m.   Evening Prayer (Every Sunday except 1st – Prayer Book liturgy (However, now it is mainly A.S.B.)
            1st Sunday – Holy Communion – Series 3

For years St James's had used the English Hymnal and chants to fit the Prayer Book Psalms and Canticles. From the beginning I dropped the singing of the Versicles and Responses and began to phase out chanting. This was done by purchasing *Psalm Praise* and using the hymns from this store, with other standard hymns to replace the Prayer Book Canticles and Psalms. The Anglican Hymn Book replaced the English Hymnal. Our stress was on congregational involvement and the maximum participation possible. Although there were ripples, if not splashes in some quarters, this plan was established and God has richly blessed us as we have met together Sunday by Sunday for worship. I, for one, find it an inspiring experience and more and more people seem to do the same as you will see from the graph showing church attendance.

The inherited situation of provision for the children on Sunday was as follows: a Sunday School took place in our Church School, some ten minutes' walk away from the church, and catered for those under eight years old. The other children were able to meet in church, with their

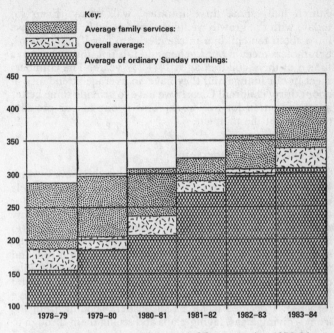

Fig. 1   Congregation numbers at 11.00 a.m. service, 1978-84

parents if they wished, for a Children's Church which began at ten a.m. Both of these had had a very useful ministry over the years.

From the beginning in the new pattern, we all worshipped at eleven a.m. together – children and adults. On the first three Sundays in the month the children left the church after about twenty minutes, for their special activities. The fourth Sunday was a Family Service. This plan was made more difficult to implement because of our lack of facilities on the church site. From the beginning we had to use the Vicarage. In those early days, when things really started to expand, we would have as many as eighty to a hundred children in the Vicarage almost every Sunday! When we found we had to use some of our bedrooms we decided it was time to move the Explorers (7–11's) and Pathfinders (11–15's) to our

church hall – some three minutes' walk away. Even so,
today, with the growth we have experienced in this area, we
have about ten children in the crèche in our 'family room';
Scramblers meet in our kitchen and it is not unusual to have
fifteen of these children aged 1½–2½ years! The Climbers
meet in our lounge and they have an average attendance of
about thirty children! Clearly we have to provide some better
accommodation for this work. This is one of our pressing
objectives at the moment.

The question of leadership

The matter of appropriate leadership for this new venture
was a vital issue. To get it wrong could jeopardise the whole
enterprise. I had to become the new Vicar of St James's, for
the sake of the people there, and I had to keep my
relationship with the folk of St Matthew's. I was going to
have to lead them into things neither group would be really
enthusiastic about, or so I thought. If I were too soft and
gentle I felt I would simply not get done what had to be done
right at the very beginning. If I were too strong and forceful
I could antagonise and spoil the possibility of a positive
response. I decided to be a real 'leader', leading from the
front – giving ideas, laying plans and seeing them through to
completion, in other words, 'managing'! At the same time I
made up my mind to be as loving, considerate and
sympathetic as possible with those who had problems,
compromising over details wherever I could.

It was a fairly lonely time for some while. I knew that, to
be biblical, I must aim to build a team of leaders. I had
inherited virtually no full-time staff. I was fortunate in
having the help of a dear lady one morning a week for the
secretarial side of things. The Verger was really an invalid
and it wasn't long before he had to move to sheltered
housing. The added complication was that in order to keep
things on an even keel, I felt I shouldn't allow the energetic
young men and women from St Matthew's to take up many
positions of leadership at St James's and thus give the
impression of a take-over. So I needed more staff, and I
needed to build a team of leaders from the whole church
body.

I had learned the importance of being extremely careful about appointing staff. I'm sure, on reflection, that the many hours spent in those early years, thinking and praying about the qualities, gifts, as well as other characteristics needed, was time well spent. The God who always provides has given us a very strong and committed team. I thank God for them all daily. What would life be without them! But where was I to start?

The finances of the church were not in great shape, as I shall show later, so I didn't have a great deal of choice. I decided that worship had to take priority. It is, after all, a 'chief duty', and certainly we all needed then, and still do, to be both inspired and enriched by worship. I had to find an organist to help to create the new vision for our worship. Once it became known that I wasn't reappointing the previous organist, who had been at the church for fifty-four years, I had quite a number of people enquiring about the post: the reason was that we have a very fine organ indeed; one of the best in London. I never had a problem getting deputies during the interregnum – I was most fortunate. But the choice of organist I knew to be crucial. The Lord was good and after about a six-month search, I was able to appoint Alan Horsey. Through his leadership we have now a strong boys' and adult choir as well as beginning to develop a special 'Family Service' Choir. We have a very competent 'Small Choir' for motets etc., as well as an orchestra and a guitar-based group. The music is truly inspiring Sunday by Sunday – this I believe has helped enormously to create a God-ward looking and positive congregation.

Then there was the teaching, preaching and Bible ministry. There was obviously a need for some further help in this area. We had a central Bible Reading at St Matthew's and there was one Bible study group at St James's when I arrived. For various reasons, I decided to have a year of Central Bible Studies, following the St Matthew's pattern; after that we would begin to form into groups. The Bishop had promised that on going to St James's I could have a Curate. This was one of my easier decisions. Tim Marshall had come to me as a student from Oak Hill Theological College, for his Sunday placement. Here was a young man of great gifts and sincere commitment. I was relieved when he said he and his wife would join us. He's been my 'Barnabas' for over five years, as well as a major contributor to the ministry and development of our church. A great number of us owe our present spiritual standing before God to his public and private ministry. Our Lord is so gracious in the way he gives us all gifts for ministry and service and then gives us opportunities to use them. He then tops that by bringing us colleagues and fellow-workers to supplement and complement our ministries.

It soon became obvious that if I was to be really serious about trying to mobilize the whole Christian Body in ministry and service, as well as cope with all the other demands, I would also need some full-time personal administrative assistance. I placed the need before the P.C.C. and suggested we made the financing of the project an extra item for the Annual Gift Day. This we did in July 1979. The money was found and six months later Miss Elizabeth Knight was appointed. My efficiency moved into a gear I had never known since my engineering days! The church quickly began to buzz as Elizabeth got to grips with the administration and communication problems that we were struggling over. Since then we've added another part-time secretary to help the team and plan shortly to buy a computer and word-processor/printer package, to help us be really professional and efficient in all our communications.

In 1983 Anne Hibbert came to join the staff team as Deaconess. Her main task was to help us with the many pastoral demands being made upon us as well as supporting the youth work in the parish. This she has already done as well as helping to launch a number of important new developments. More about this later.

Of course 'staff' does not equal 'leadership' of a church. Our church is fortunate in having people of rich leadership potential. This we have endeavoured to tap and develop by running training courses and laying aside time to talk to people specifically about their gifts, their use and development. Ever since I first read Howard Snyder's book *New Wineskins* and later, *The Community of the King*, I've realised the importance of good working structures to help and encourage involvement and leadership development. We have always tried to be a 'Parish Church' with a 'parochial' ministry, but have understood that for such to grow and develop we need to establish, and continually expand, a firm base of Christian leadership. This we have tried to do while using the traditional Anglican structures and building upon them. So, with our two church wardens, who are truly spiritual leaders in our church and to whom I look, we have created a network of co-leaders. Assistant churchwardens lead the teams of sidesmen and deal with the usual tasks connected with running Sunday worship. Another assistant warden is responsible for all matters relating to the fabric of the church – a key figure in our church. Our Treasurer is also a highly respected member. He too sees the importance of delegation and runs a 'department' with some thirty-five different people involved in looking after the financial affairs of the church!

We've tried to look back and plot developments. Now as I look around our church and fellowship today, what features stand out that haven't already been mentioned?

1. *Newcomers.* We are fortunate in having a regular trickle of new people coming to worship with us Sunday by Sunday. This isn't due to a highly sophisticated publicity campaign – for some considerable time we didn't even have a notice outside the church giving details of services! These newcomers to our worship are not due either to a comprehensive evangelistic outreach to the parish, though this isn't to say we're not involved in publicity or evangelism, for we are. We have a very keen group of 'evangelists' who go out into the parish from time to time. I am sure, however, that quite a proportion of our newcomers have been brought to worship by a friend or relative. One other major factor in attracting people must be the position of the church and its elegance. We have a most attractive building with a very tall spire and are doubly fortunate in being placed at the very heart of the shopping area and centre of Muswell Hill. There is a sizeable percentage of our community that is mobile. People are coming and going all the time. Some of these are Christians moving in and quickly looking for a place of worship – the building is so prominent it's natural for them to look in on us. It is however worth noting here some figures that show the parochial nature of the church:

Distance from church	Percentage of congregation
½ mile	44 %
up to 1 mile	40 %
1–2 miles	11 %
over 2 miles	5 %

By and large the newcomers to our church are similarly within a radius of a mile or so, and this feature has encouraged us to set up a team of people to look after this part of our ministry, under the leadership of a young Australian couple, themselves fairly new, together with our Deaconess.

As newcomers come to St James's on a Sunday, they are, we hope, welcomed and made to feel at home, and, over a cup of coffee at the back of the church, introduced to others. At the same time they are encouraged to complete a Welcome card and hand it to the Vicar. A record is made in the office of their name and address and the card is passed to our team. One of them then visits the newcomer and also invites him or her to an informal social event in the home of a team member, with special refreshments. Each newcomer may well be invited to several such social events which we hope will broaden their circle of friends within the life of our church. In this way, when they come to church there are familiar faces.

During the course of each term we have at least one Open House in the Vicarage. By now the newcomers will, we hope, be at ease in the setting and I take the opportunity of telling them more about what goes on at St James's and encourage them to get involved in our Starters Fellowship or a Bible Study Fellowship Group. In the following weeks as they are drawn into, and become more committed to, the life and work of the church, they are then invited to a Mini-Stewardship Lunch. These also take place once a term. Usually a person will have been coming to St James's for several months before being invited to this lunch. On each such occasion the principles of Christian Stewardship are clearly explained. All those attending the lunch are later visited by members of our team of Stewardship Visitors, when they are urged to offer themselves for some task in the church according to their gifts and abilities. At the same time they are encouraged to assess their giving to the church and to be realistic in that – and where possible to covenant that giving. To date about ninety per cent of regular giving is covenanted.

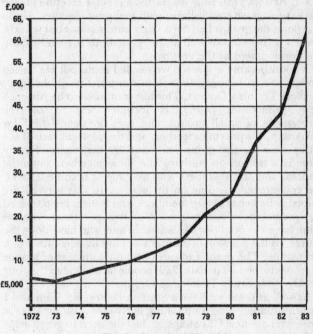

Fig. 2   Income, 1972–83

For a number of years now we have been trying to develop this structure and pastoral ministry for helping newcomers to become integrated into the life of the church. We are most encouraged by its effectiveness and we are now looking at other areas of our work that need similar attention.

2. *Bible Study Fellowship Groups.* When I arrived in 1978 there was one Bible study group. For a year we moved to a Central Bible Study and prayer meeting. When we eventually went back into groups we were able to form four,

meeting weekly. We tried periodic 'Central' meetings, but these only attracted the minority of group members. It then dawned on us that the central meeting for Christians was worship on Sunday. By 1981 the number of groups had risen to six. At about this time we started a regular meeting for the leaders when we could share, plan and pray together. Up to this point the groups had been fairly autonomous but we now started to have an overall strategy for both the studies and the development of the groups.

It soon became apparent we needed more but we lacked leaders. So in January 1982 Tim ran our first Bible Study Leaders Training Course. This has continued to be run each term (sometimes twice). It includes sessions on the importance of small groups; the need for leadership, for fellowship, for praying together; and the pastoral care of the group both by the group itself and by the leader. Finally there is a session on studying the Bible together. Potential leaders, and also members who may never become leaders, are encouraged to come on the course. In this way all are helped to be better group members, and leaders are prepared for leadership in due course. We often put those who we think have the qualities of leadership and who have done the course, in the position of assistant or joint leaders of a group for a while. The graph indicates how the numbers of groups have developed. To date 280 people are involved in our weekly Bible Study Fellowship Groups.

As well as these we have a Starters Fellowship. Tim and I host this limited-life group lasting for twelve sessions; it is for those who are new Christians, or feel the need to get to grips with the basics of the faith. It is mainly didactic in nature, but as the term progresses the group is helped to share together and to pray together. In this way they are prepared for group membership, which for many of them is a completely new concept.

The Curate took over responsibility for these Fellowship Groups about a year ago, and now during each term he arranges to see leaders in threes and fours in order to share ideas, plan and pray together and help over problems. Then once a term all the leaders meet together in the Vicarage for an open time of sharing and planning. On these occasions I usually speak at the end of the evening, seeking to give some

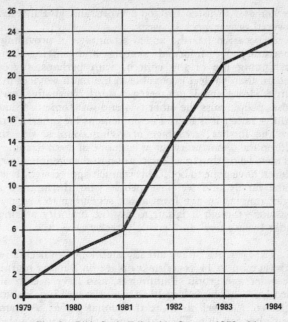

Fig. 3   Bible Study Fellowship Groups, 1979–84

help and encouragement, both spiritually and practically, to these leaders in this shared ministry within the life and work of the church.

3. *'Sunday Night'*. Now that the church congregation is so large, it is easy for individuals to become lost in the crowd. Apart from urging people to become closely involved in one group or another, we have started 'Sunday Night'. This takes place in the Vicarage on Sundays following the evening service. It acts as a kind of half-way house from the large group, in the church, and the very small housegroups. Between forty and sixty people come along each week to share together. It provides an opportunity for individuals to express particular concerns for prayer, to share something they have learned recently, to bring a word of encouragement to the group, and for the group to pray

together and to listen to God's Word and give thanks for answered prayer week by week.

This occasion has the added advantage of providing an opportunity for informal sharing and singing in the worshipping life of the church, with perhaps a greater freedom than we feel is possible in the main services in the church. However it is not seen as a third, alternative service, so that people miss the other two and just come to 'Sunday Night' – rather it is there to complement the others. It does have the further advantage of giving couples with small children the opportunity for at least one of them to come out and have fellowship in a larger group in the evening after the children have gone to bed! This is much appreciated. It is for all the family and we have people who are married and single, ranging in age from about seventeen to seventy on occasions – though it is fair to say the majority are in the 'under twenty-five' and 'single' brackets.

4. *Teenagers*. As I have already mentioned, our children's work (age up to 14 years) takes place on Sunday morning. The older age group, Pathfinders, also have a club night called Link-2. This is largely an activities evening, including crafts, etc., as well as more traditional games. A team of about nine run this. The programme also includes a simple epilogue at some point. About thirty attend. Some of these are the children of church families, but a number are their friends in the local schools and have little or no Christian background.

The next stage up from Link-2 is Clubnight for the over fourteens – again an activities evening with an epilogue, and about forty attend. In addition they have Soapbox which happens on another occasion. This is an opportunity for serious discussion about the Christian faith and about thirty come along to that and it's a lively occasion! Again, most have little Christian background.

In all these activities, Link-2, Clubnight and Soapbox, our Deaconess has led and co-ordinated events and the teams, and has been instrumental also in developing much of what is happening (though Clubnight had been started before her arrival). With both teams of leaders Anne has spent considerable time, helping them and praying with them.

Prior to holidays away with the children which she has also arranged, she has taken the leaders away on separate training weekends at which she and other gifted members of the church have taken sessions. These have been enormously beneficial as they have provided an opportunity to get to know one another more deeply and to share and pray together for the young people they seek to win for the Lord.

5. *Missionary support and giving.* For some years now we have been conscious of the lack of lively missionary support. In October 1981 the Missionary Committee was reactivated and has met regularly ever since. The church supports, to a greater or lesser degree, six different mission groups or individuals. Each month one of these is featured as a Missionary Focus in the parish magazine, in the weekly noticesheet, in the Sunday prayers and also with a large display at the back of the church. Each group has one person who is responsible for liaison, publicity and displays, etc. But as well as that, each of our fellowship groups is linked with one or another of these missions in an attempt to foster mission interest, particularly among those in the church who have never had contact with missions and missionaries before.

Historically the church has for over seventy years supported one school in South India and has had a Christmas sale each year without a break – the proceeds of which have gone solely to that school. We now have no other sales or fairs to raise money. The Missionary Committee put forward a proposal which was quickly adopted and is proving very successful. Each month we make available some extra offering envelopes marked 'My donation for this month's Missionary Focus'. Anyone wishing to contribute to that particular mission or missionary, merely puts that money into one of these and slips it into the offering with their normal giving. This scheme has been in operation since October 1983 and each month has seen a significant figure being donated through that means.

As well as this, the P.C.C. came to the realisation in 1981 that if we are encouraging the individuals in the church to tithe their income, then we as a church should do the same. As a result of these two developments the church's giving to mission, both at home and broad, has increased from 1975–83 by 450 per cent.

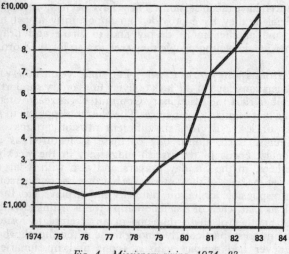

Fig. 4   Missionary giving, 1974–83.

Each year we have a Missionary Weekend which includes special speakers on Sunday, and recently we have had a highly successful family occasion on the Saturday evening, entitled International Evening, to which about 100 have come and shared both food and entertainment from different nations, as well as drama and singing – all with a mission theme.

It is exciting to see that we have now four or five people seriously considering full-time service either at home or abroad.

Conclusions

Over the past few years I have been greatly stimulated and helped by a number of friends, as I have sought to serve the church here. I also benefited enormously from a visit to Fuller Theological Seminary, Pasadena, California, U.S.A., in 1982. More recently I attended the first International Clergy School run by the Institute of Contemporary Christianity. What an exciting new development in in-service training for pastors and leaders this is.

Knowing what I know now I think there are a number of things I might have tackled differently in those early days at St Matthew's. I should, I think, have spent more of my time training people for leadership and building small groups. I was very negligent and slow in these areas. It wouldn't have been easy, but on reflection something more could have been done in these key areas. I have also come to realise that in church growth 'bigger' is not necessarily 'better' – it's certainly not 'easier', I can testify to that. In our much larger church now there is a great deal that is extremely encouraging and exciting. There is fruit to be seen, for which we praise God. As we have grown we have tried to help our fellowship to shoulder pastoral responsibilities. We are most fortunate in having so many gifted and caring people.

However, there is still constant pressure – for as the church has grown, so the pressures have grown too. What is this pressure? In 2 Corinthians 11:23–27, Paul speaks of his sufferings and concludes in verses 28 and 29: 'Besides everything else, I face daily the pressure of my concern for all the churches. Who is weak, and I do not feel weak? Who is led into sin, and I do not inwardly burn?' Our 'concerns' are much more humble and modest compared with those of the great Apostle, for we have only one church, but this church has grown, and the pastoral responsibilities have grown with it.

Some need to find Christ – all need to become 'mature in Christ'. All come with a contribution to make to the life of our church, but all need to be trained and all have needs of one kind or another. While we teach and preach about mutual responsibility and the 'one another' ministries – like 'burden-bearing', 'encouragement', etc., there is in practice a time lag. Not every person who joins a caring group is quickly 'adopted', and of course there are some who may never join a group. This means that while we have a large percentage of people in such groups, the real pastoral weight carried by the staff is quite considerable. The problem I believe is that Christians, and I mean all of us, are rather slow at taking on extra responsibilities. Clearly then, the pastor of a growing church has to find more and more time for people and has to look for more pastors to help him, if the church isn't going to become superficial and unloving. This is a major challenge that faces us today. For me personally, the words of the Apostle Paul recorded in Acts 20:28 are especially challenging: 'Guard yourselves,' he says to the elders, 'and all the flock of which the Holy Spirit has made you overseers. Be shepherds of the Church of God . . .'

Chapter 4

Above Bar Church, Southampton

David Jackman

Above Bar Church, which is affiliated to the Fellowship of Independent Evangelical Churches, is situated in Southampton city centre, in the main shopping street. The congregation is drawn from every area of the city (roughly 75% living within three miles of the church building, which corresponds to the city boundary).

There are two Sunday morning services, each with adult attendances of around 350, and an evening congregation of around 650. These figures compare with about 400 attending in 1978.

The minister is David Jackman, who leads a staff team of four. David was born in Bournemouth and grew up in a Christian family: he graduated with a degree in English from Downing College, Cambridge, where he was involved in the leadership of the university Christian Union. After a post-graduate certificate in education at Exeter he taught at Portsmouth Grammar School, and then joined the staff of the Universities and Colleges Christian Fellowship (then IVF) as Universities' Secretary.

Six years of service in universities throughout the UK were followed by two years of theological study at Trinity College, Bristol, and in 1976 David joined Leith Samuel, first as assistant and then, in 1978, as associate minister at Above Bar, succeeding him in 1980.

He met his wife Heather, a dietitian, through Crusaders, and they have two children.

Above Bar Church was founded in 1876 and has been on its present city-centre site for over a hundred years. Originally it was the product of the ministry of an American evangelist, Henry Earl, who came to Britain with the intention of founding Church of Christ congregations in this country. Where better to start than in the busy transatlantic port where he docked? So the church began with strong evangelical foundations, although it became independent of its American origins before the First World War. About that time, Fredrick Phillips began a long ministry of over forty years, which was followed in 1953 by Leith Samuel, so that the church had only two ministers between 1911 and 1980, both of them clearly evangelical and thoroughly biblical. Today we stand on other men's shoulders.

A new building

Before the Second World War, there was a good deal of housing around the church building, which had itself been erected in 1880. But the blitz put an end to that, and at the height of the bombing only the church and the cinema next door were left standing. The new Southampton centre that arose from the ashes was a utilitarian structure of the 1950s, with shops and offices but not homes. The congregation was scattered throughout the city, but the centrality of the building and comparative ease of transport meant that the church continued to be well-attended, and the years after the war and into the fifties often saw large congregations. Changing its name from 'Church of Christ' to 'Above Bar Church', the church became known as a centre of evangelical life and witness in the area.

As the post-war economy developed, so did the pressures on the church to leave its prime commercial site and be rehoused in a brand new plant on the outskirts of the city ('where nobody could get to us' as one church leader remarked). These overtures were strongly resisted. Well over a dozen approaches were received in the sixties and seventies from developers interested in claiming the ground, which the church was sure had been God's provision. 'In these days of declining attendances, we are sure you will want to capitalise on your resources . . . ' There was a depressing familiarity about the assumptions, but the church leaders still held to the site as a trust from God. Had not he preserved the building and the living church through the war?

However, the building was showing distinct signs of wear and the war damage had clearly weakened the structure. Successive modernisation plans had done what they could to update the facilities, but the building remained what it always had been, a typical Victorian chapel, long and thin, with a three-sided gallery and, at the back, 'rooms'. The discovery of rot in the roof in the mid-seventies led the church officers to a detailed survey of the whole fabric, which in turn revealed that over the next few years well over £100,000 would have to be spent on the building to keep it usable. Was that a right expenditure? About the same time, one particularly persistent developer came up with a new scheme, to put shops at the street level and rehouse the church above it, with a major entrance on the main street, which had always been a stipulation of the church officers before any plan would be considered. Was this God's answer to the congregation's prayers? It proved to be so.

On 1 July 1979, the last morning service was broadcast from the old building on local radio and at that evening's Communion service we covenanted together 'to stay close to the Lord and to one another', while we were away from the site. The next week the bulldozers moved in, and from that moment the church started to grow. On Sundays we met in two different locations. In the morning we used the largest lecture theatre in the new University Medical School, and with it the concourse area for children's groups and seminar rooms for the crèche and teenagers. The evenings saw us in the theatre of the local College of Higher Education, back in the city centre, only a few hundred yards from our own site.

The most noticeable immediate change was within the church fellowship. In the old building, the gallery had emptied from two side exits and the downstairs from the main front doors. There was a very small and cramped vestibule, so that any mixing was usually done on the pavement, though refreshments were sometimes available at the rear of the building. Now the whole bag had been shaken up. People could no longer sit in the same seats as they had done for years and church members began to discover one another. The new surroundings were secular, but modern and attractive. A few newcomers began to attend, who freely admitted that they would never have visited the old building, and we were beginning to learn that while the church is not a building, nevertheless bricks and mortar can have an enormous effect on any church's life.

For two years and two months the church was away from its site, learning all sorts of invaluable lessons, especially that of adaptability. For the rebuilding project, we were greatly blessed in our choice of architect, Robert Potter, a committed Christian, who had recently completed the restructuring of All Souls, Langham Place, in the heart of London. Robert's skill and ingenuity have been of untold benefit in the growth of the church ever since. His ability to use the limited space creatively was an asset of incalculable worth.

Two shops are at street level, along with the main church entrance. The church comprises three floors above and half of the basement area. On arrival the visitor is taken by lift or stairs to the first floor, where a large lounge with refreshment facilities, books, etc., feeds into the main church worship area. This is based on an amphitheatre model, with the seating grouped around the pulpit and Communion table, under a hexagonal ceiling, and gently tiered towards the gallery, which sweeps along one side of the building and extends above the lounge. There is seating for 650 in this area. Behind the gallery there is a well-equipped crèche and above it the main church hall, with a kitchen designed to serve cooked meals for 120 people. Accommodation on the three floors at the rear of the building provides office, vestry, committee and classroom facilities, while the basement has provided a natural focus for our young people's groups. Apart from the basement, all the accommodation is carpeted and great care was taken with the decor, so that the most attractive and comfortable furnishings might be provided, without extravagance. The basic building was provided to the church by the developers, but the congregation has raised almost £250,000 in five years to cover its equipment and furnishing. This in itself has been a story of generous giving and immense encouragement to our corporate faith.

Two factors in our growth

A new church building, the first in living memory in the city-centre, is itself news, and we certainly benefited from the attention of the local media, with which continuing good relationships have been established. The growth that had begun in a small way while we were out of the building rapidly accelerated when we came into our new premises. It's difficult to know how important the building has been in this, but many of our new Christians have told me that they would never have given a thought to entering the old church. From the start, we have tried to welcome people, to invite them to look around and to have a cup of coffee. Most Saturday mornings we run an open-house coffee shop and this has been extended at Christmas or on special city occasions, such as when the Tall Ships race ended in Southampton. This has proved to be a valuable ice-breaker to many people, of all ages, who would normally have found the experience of crossing a church threshold quite foreign and even threatening.

But none of this would have been of any value without the warmth of the church members themselves. We are utterly convinced that initial impressions are vital and we have really had to work hard on this. We now always welcome 'first-timers' publicly, at every service, and explain how to find your way to the Information Desk, or to coffee. A team of couples (from twenties to fifties) staff the desk which carries all the information about different activities within the church. Coffee and tea are served after each main service, and church members are especially encouraged not to let any newcomer leave without a friendly welcome and an invitation to coffee. Of course, some visitors still do slip through, but with members of the leadership team on the lookout for newcomers and everyone doing their bit, more and more people tell us that the warmth and sincerity of the welcome has been a major factor in their coming back.

The other major factor has been the central ingredient of expository biblical teaching, which has been a feature of the church for some time. So many different definitions of biblical exposition exist today that it may be as well to define this a little more closely. Our practice is to be going through a book of the Bible, or a definite section of Scripture (e.g. the Sermon on the Mount) in the mornings, and another in the evening services. In shaping this pattern, there are some vital ingredients to consider. There needs to be a balanced diet, both between Old and New Testaments and in terms of the type of material covered – narrative, doctrinal, poetic, etc. The biblical material itself should dictate the pace at which the exposition proceeds; but no series should be too long. It is much better to break off and return to one of the larger books than to soldier on to the (bitter?) end. At the time of writing, we are dealing with the second half of Ephesians over three months on Sunday mornings, at an average rate of six or seven verses a week, while in the evenings we are studying Exodus 1–19, from the birth of Moses to Sinai, in the same period of time.

Expository preaching is only boring when the pace is too slow. Personally, I do not favour the sort of sermon which concentrates on one verse, from which is wrung out all the systematic theology that can be detected, with scant reference to the context and very little overview of the whole sweep of the argument or direction of the book. That seems to me to be more imposition than exposition! But real biblical exposition over the years teaches a congregation the balance of Scripture, avoids ministerial hobby-horses and develops the sort of corporate church mind that is prepared to accept change, when it can be demonstrated to be biblical. That has been a really important factor in our own accommodation to change, as a growing church. One further essential is that such preaching should be applied. God's truth sown in the mind must warm the heart, in order to activate the will. Too much so-called 'biblical exposition' is inexcusably academic and narrowly cerebral. But the Bible itself is never like that. We need to apply that truth to the everyday situations our congregations are facing and to teach them how to put the lessons they learn into practice. The New Testament epistles arose out of practical Christian living in a pagan world and the sort of urgent problems it threw up. Significantly, its doctrinal content arises out of those real-life situations, so that its applications are always on target. Biblical preaching must reflect biblical patterns, by which I mean that there should be no imperatives without

the indicatives, no commands without promises, no challenges without the divine resources being revealed. We must
appeal to the whole man and apply the whole counsel of God
to his total situation. All our researches show that biblical
teaching of this sort has been a major factor in our growth,
and not just by transfer (there has been comparatively little
of that) but biologically and by conversion.

In this context, it is worth stating that a church members'
meeting, soon after we moved into the new building,
established two priorities by which everything else in the life
of the church was to be assessed. These were evangelism and
edification, or making and maturing disciples. There is
nothing remarkable in identifying these as the central
concerns of a biblical church, but we have found this agreed
affirmation invaluable as a touchstone of our planning and
decision-making. It still amazes me how little of our energy,
time and money are actually channelled into these
fundamental areas, but no church can begin to grow without
commitment to such priorities. They have helped us not to
set an artificial ceiling on our growth, not to be dictated to by
the restrictions of our building and not to allow such
tempting considerations as our personal comfort, or our
traditions, to side-track us from God's plans. Of course
people had begun to say, 'The church is big enough.' In
1978 the average congregation size on an equivalent Sunday
had been around four hundred at each service; now it was
creeping up towards seven hundred. A full building can be a
great inspiration in worship, but it can also be very
inconvenient and make people feel pressurised. It was
hardest for those who had been in the church for some years
and who had got to know 'everybody', but who now found it
impossible to keep up with all the newcomers. Indeed, that
has been one of the most difficult things for many of the
members who have been at Above Bar for some years to
accept. It's not a factor of age, I have discovered, but of
personal security and the readiness to view change
positively. Some of the oldest members have been among the
most enthusiastic about the developments!

Surveying the congregation

Within a year of moving into the new building, we had

noticed two major effects. The Sunday morning congregation was regularly overflowing the accommodation, so that the TV relay was always in use. Newcomers might enjoy the novelty for a week or two, but it was no way permanently to welcome them. We ran a rota system by which church members sat in the relay, first on an alphabetical basis and then by house groups, but it was becoming clear that the physical constraints of the building were actually hindering our growth. We were committed to sharing the gospel with the city, but in effect the message to a visitor was 'There's no room for you here.' In addition, the growth was already causing the organisational structures of the church to creak alarmingly. The full-time team of three was at full stretch and the church office, which had been opened (mornings only) with the new building, was snowed under. In situations like this lots of people have all sorts of remedies, of which some are more realistic than others! Ours is a congregational system of church government, so that all major policy decisions ultimately depend upon the agreement of the members' meeting. I have always been committed to involving as many members as possible in the decision-making process and we have devised an 'open forum' approach when important decisions have to be taken. The basic idea is to provide a discussion meeting, where everyone knows no vote will be taken, in which the church can meet to share views, assess opinions, sieve ideas and generally seek a clearer understanding of issues involved and the possible ways forward. The leadership has a very important input to occasions like this, but the listening role is equally vital, and we have found this approach has really helped us in working for a consensus.

To achieve that end, we decided to hold a congregational survey, devised and analysed for us by Peter Brierley, an old friend of the church, then of the Bible Society and now of MARC Europe. Accordingly, on the last Sunday of November 1982, all those attending the services were asked to indicate their preference for various future courses of action related to these challenges. The results showed 41% in favour of extending the relay system and 42% in favour of having two morning services, with 11% uncertain and 6% advocating no action for the time being. Looking back we can see God's hand in that. The church was so clearly divided that we had to give ourselves to a protracted period of prayer and discussion on the whole matter. Had the voting been much more uneven it would have been tempting for the majority group to want to steamroller the others into its own favoured solution, with potentially harmful and disruptive results.

But the most valuable spin-off of the exercise was the profile of the church which we are able to draw, defined by the characteristics requested on the questionnaire. We discovered that we have approximately equal numbers attending in each of the age bands 19–21, 22–29, 30–44 and 45–64, despite the differing widths of these bands. The numbers are untypical of Hampshire churches as a whole, especially within the 19–29 age group, and very dissimilar to the population as a whole. The average age of the congregation is 38, as compared with 41 on a smaller survey in 1969. Another interesting statistic was that 32% had been coming to the church for less than a year, 34% between 2 and 10 years and 34% over 11 years (18% of the total attending for more than 20 years). The congregation divided into 46% male and 54% female, the mix varying by age group. There are more men than women coming in their twenties and a higher-than-average proportion in their thirties and early forties, which are very unusual occurrences in church life. Virtually half the attenders (49%) are single; 42% are married, the remaining 9% being widowed, or divorced. There are proportionately twice as many single people attending the church as in the general population, which is partly explained by the considerable number of students.

City-centre churches like Above Bar are often accused of importing people from great distances and so weakening more local congregations. While it is true that some do travel many miles, the survey helped to get this issue into perspective. Almost half the congregation travel under two miles to church and three-quarters less than three miles, which corresponds with the city boundary. It had been suggested that another congregation should be planted as the solution to the overcrowding problem, but there is already an evangelical witness in every main area of the city. Some have suggested that many travel in from outside the city and that another church should be started in one of these areas, but the actual numbers coming from these areas do not give substantial ground for this argument.

Another helpful question explored how people had first been introduced to the church. A number of alternatives were suggested, and many wrote in additional items, but the two main reasons were a personal involvement, either through family or a friend's invitation (59%), and the church's reputation for biblical preaching (47%). The whole panorama of church activities, although they are clearly essential for developing and maintaining established contact, actually drew in relatively few in the first instance. We also enquired what had been most helpful in people coming to feel part of the church family. Several suggestions were made and there was no one clear reason. But the warmth of fellowship, involvement in activities and the stimulus of the home-based Prayer and Bible Groups figured highly in the list. There were 96 people who described themselves as 'visitors' that day, 11% of the total congregation, while 7% of the total were not yet 'sure that I am a Christian'.

Handling growth

A year of discussion, prayer and feasibility studies followed the questionnaire. During that time numbers were still increasing, but at a slower rate than in the preceding year. Gradually it was becoming clear that two Sunday morning services was the only way forward, if we were to allow for continuing growth. It was a great encouragement to us all that the members' meeting which decided to go ahead with that did so with no votes against and only four abstentions, just about a year after the questionnaire was issued. In fact the meeting insisted on changing the original wording of the motion which spoke of the 'problem' of overcrowding to the 'opportunity'! To move ahead with that degree of unanimity and purpose was well worth the painstaking process of consultation and patient explanation. From January 1984 we have held two morning services at nine-thirty and eleven a.m. Both have the same teaching content, with the same preacher, though the worship is led by different people and may vary. The earlier service has the children's and Junior Church ingredient, to resist the gravitational pull of the traditional eleven a.m. slot. But the latter has a wide range of ages, the younger single people preferring the later starting time! The congregation divided almost equally between the two, without any direction. Many have sampled both, but most settle quickly to a preference, although I suspect nine-thirty may be especially popular on sunny summer days. The result has been an accelerated and noticeable growth in attendance at both services, which has also spilt over into Sunday evenings where we are just beginning to reach the sort of overcrowding situation and TV relay system we faced on Sunday mornings. Much thought and prayer are currently being given to this challenge. Two evening services would perhaps be a rather unimaginative response and we may well begin to provide some alternative learning groups, not exactly the all-age Sunday schools which are widespread in the U.S.A., but some particular course options to which perhaps a couple of hundred people might commit themselves over, say, a ten-week block. All this is very tentative at present, but it is good to be facing continuing challenges and opportunities of this sort, which force us to think freshly about the way we organise.

Growth is a complicated phenomenon and it is easy to be side-tracked by numbers. Heaven counts roots rather than heads, and I am aware that a great deal of energy and resources can be devoured by the demands of those who are, at best, on the periphery of church life. The danger with a growing church is that it can attract newcomers for the wrong reasons. Some people just like to join what looks like a going concern, but they are often temperamentally 'getters' rather than 'givers'. Whatever size a church may be, it seems to be an invariable and biblical rule that there are never sufficient labourers (Matt. 9:37). People look at a large church and either decide 'there's nothing here for me to do', or worse still, 'they are all far more capable than I am'. But they are very often the people who are most needed.

Much of our recent growth, however, has been either through totally unchurched people coming to Christ, or those with a church background which has lapsed, coming to a personal faith. There have been transfers from other

churches, but these are mainly people moving into
Southampton from elsewhere, rather than from within the
city. This is probably because the whole spectrum of church
life is currently represented in the city, so that Christians can
usually settle into a congenial church situation comparatively
easily.

We are certainly not interested in filling seats with 'come
and sit and watch' Christians. Our concern is to build a
family of Christians who 'come and work and share', whose
fellowship and service are the daily expression of their
learning and worship. I am sure there is no human formula
that can produce this. 'Only God makes things grow' (1 Cor.
3:7). What we have tried to do is to develop helpful
structures which focus our energies and skills in the areas of
making and maturing disciples, which we have identified as
God-given priorities.

The centrality of prayer

Central to this has been our concern to involve as many
people as possible in the prayer ministry of the church. We
have a small but committed prayer chain, contacted by
telephone, who are prepared at any time to pray intensively
about specific, often emergency, needs. A much larger
number use the daily prayer guide, produced monthly. Until
1983 a weekly prayer meeting was held, but we were
concerned that many of our new Christians and young
people found it difficult to participate in a rather formal
gathering of around a hundred people. So this year we have
put our prayer focus into the fortnightly housegroups, now
renamed Prayer and Bible Groups, where there is a detailed
duplicated list of prayer topics available for the leaders, as
well as notes and questions on the Bible passage, which all
the groups study. In this way, each of the groups is covering
the same material and there is a greater sense of unity, but
many will pray audibly in a small group much more easily.

On the other weeks, we all meet together for 'Church
Night', which is held centrally, in the church. This is a more
relaxed time of worship, news sharing, fellowship and
prayer, and seems to be drawing almost as many as the
housegroups. Here we often break down into smaller groups

of five or six for prayer. Doing this means that far more people are aware of the church's prayer needs and actually involved in praying them through at any given time. They are also much better informed about our church missionaries, who are featured regularly in rotation, and about planning new developments. Church Night attenders sense their involvement in the life of the fellowship; this has been a major factor in newcomers taking that all-important step of involvement, which stops thinking about the church as 'them' and starts thinking about 'us'. None of us is fully aware how much we owe to the secret, unheralded prayer ministry, faithfully exercised every day by some of our older members who are unable now to be physically involved. It is undoubtedly a huge, hidden benefit.

New Christians

As a church, we are learning to be outward looking, always reaching out, always trying to include new people, developing the sort of corporate attitude that is delighted to see other people come in. That's important in every group that meets, as well as on Sundays. Christians who develop the attitude 'It's *our* church and we don't want anybody else taking it over' have to be lovingly but firmly rebuked. As Archbishop William Temple put it, 'The Christian church is the only society that exists for those who are not yet its members.' But, of course, to many, church-going is a totally unknown experience. We have tried to overcome this by having regular Guest Services, in which the whole approach is designed to present the claims of Christ in the most relevant way possible. From those services we are looking for those in whom the Holy Spirit is at work and who express a desire to take things further. By far the most fruitful evangelistic tool we have used over the past three years has been a small discussion group, which we call 'Christian Basics', where nothing is assumed and no questions are barred. This five-week course, led by a couple in their home, covers such areas as 'How do we know there's a God?' 'What is he like?' 'Who was Jesus?' 'What's gone wrong with the world?' 'Why did Jesus die?' 'Did he really rise again?' and 'What does being a Christian involve?' God has used this to bring many, of all ages, to faith. It has also been encouraging to see a wide social spread in these groups, so that the church continues to be a cross-section of the city as a whole.

New Christians are encouraged to attend a longer, twelve-week course, called 'Learn Your Faith'. This is a mix of basic doctrine, practical help in getting started in Christian living, fellowship and worship, with plenty of opportunities for questions and answers. Groups are usually small (six to eight) and personal contact is an important ingredient. Further small group involvement is then strongly encouraged as an essential element of continuing growth. For the under twenty-fives, this may be through one of the youth groups, and for the over twenty-fives, through the Prayer and Bible Groups which meet fortnightly, in homes, all round the city. These groups are the building blocks of the infrastructure and their leadership is a key role in the church's life. They tend to provide homogeneous units, because they are geographically selected, and in a city like ours different areas of housing tend to focus age and social factors. This is a great strength in a widely diverse congregation, where naturally a newcomer is on the lookout for 'my sort of people'. We have tried to resist pressures to sub-divide by age, although a fortnightly Luncheon Fellowship, for the retired, has proved to be not only a much-appreciated fellowship focus, but a very useful introduction to the church. Otherwise we do all we can to keep families together and focus on the home as the basic church unit.

After a while, newcomers are invited to tea on a Sunday at the church to meet one another and some of the staff team and deacons, with their families. On that occasion we highlight and explain the major church activities and encourage them to attend a short series of three classes on baptism and church membership. At the same time they are invited to fill in an Involvement Questionnaire, which explains something like fifty areas of church life where a contribution can be made – from hospitality to flower-arranging, from electronics to cooking, from visitation evangelism to baby-sitting. This information constitutes a reservoir of skills and gifts, always available in the church office, on which we continually draw in the everyday life of the church family. It is thrilling to see many new converts already playing their part in stewarding, serving coffee, distributing leaflets and a score of other ways.

Discipleship training

However, it has become apparent that we shall need a continual flow of well-equipped workers, in order to facilitate and cope with continual growth. To meet this need we have adopted a two-year course, prepared by the Navigators, called the 2:7 Series – Discipleship Training for Church Laymen. This is based on the priorities of Colossians 2:7, 'Rooted and built up in him, strengthened in the faith as you were taught, and overflowing with thankfulness.' Designed and used in the U.S.A over the last ten years, this course has now been introduced into Britain. Above Bar is among the first group of churches to use it and currently we have over fifty people involved. The course is taught weekly, over six twelve-week terms, in groups of six to ten, and aims to help each person become a mature disciple of Jesus Christ and to equip him or her with the tools and know-how to make disciples of others. We are currently looking forward to the first three groups completing the course this summer, and from then on a steady flow of well-equipped couples and individuals becoming available to staff our evangelistic and nurturing groups, as well as others being involved in different church activities.

The other lesson we have learned about the training and utilisation of gifts, within the fellowship, is that this does not become possible without an adequate level of full-time staffing. Historically the full-time ministry in our sort of church has rested with one man, and that has often proved to be a real bottle-neck. I became convinced of the biblical nature of a team ministry which provides training, and we have gradually enlarged our team. Last autumn we were able to make a new appointment of a full-time assistant minister for pastoral care and counselling. As a trained biblical counsellor, his role is both to pastor and train others, and already we are greatly benefiting from his input. In addition, we have an assistant minister, who shares in most aspects of the work including preaching, but whose major pastoral responsibility is the young people, and also a lady assistant.

We all do too much administration, and having recently commissioned an evaluation study of the church's management, we are currently discussing how this burden can best be shared and the whole process streamlined. Old traditions change slowly, but the creaking of the structures is making plain even to the most conservative among us that our growth means that change is no longer merely an option, but an essential. It's not always easy for the church members to understand why the minister's role has to change, but we are beginning to see that the traditional functions have to be shared out more widely, if we are to avoid the frustrations of the ministerial bottle-neck.

One potential problem we have identified is that of the full-time staff team wanting to move ahead more quickly than the part-time lay leadership. Because the staff are in day-to-day contact with a large variety of situations and needs, it is much easier for them to have an overview of the whole church life. However, if they are either fairly new to the church or comparatively young, it is not always easy for the elected officers to have confidence in their judgement. In a period of growth, it is easy for an accelerator – brake effect to develop. The same mechanism can be observed in some churches which have implemented a two-tier system of deacons and elders. The elders are often just that – considerably older, whereas the deacons may be younger men, full of drive, energy and enthusiasm for change, but lacking in experience (the one fault that time will infallibly cure!).

The answer, if the church is not to judder and shudder from alternate use of accelerator and brake, is to develop the sense of partnership and of interdependence among all the leaders. We need to know each other really well, so that we love and respect one another. We need to pray together frequently and work for consensus as determinedly as possible. We need to seek unanimity, without ever making it such an inflexible requirement that one man can exercise a virtual veto. We are currently learning together in these areas, and the experience is both challenging and exciting.

One of the great gifts we treasure in Above Bar is the large measure of unity God has given us and the ability actually to agree to differ over peripheral matters – but still to agree, as members of the one family.

A bright future

The future is, of course, quite unknown, but it is as bright as God's promises. We do not believe that there is any reason why the church should not continue to grow, but in saying that we recognise that all growth is God's gracious initiative and we are utterly dependent on him. The moment we begin to imagine we have a right formula, or that we somehow deserve God's blessing, or that any spiritual 'technology' can produce life, is the moment we begin to contract, to atrophy and to perish. 'Only God makes things grow' and that includes churches! A church like Above Bar has considerable potential for penetration in a city like Southampton. Of those to whom much is given, much will be required.

One of the most encouraging features of the last two years has been the growing fellowship and co-operation between evangelical Christians from many churches in the city, recognising that we all have different roles to play. Larger churches may be able to provide nurture and encouragement, but they also have a responsibility to encourage other fellowships, by providing lay preachers and the resource people, and perhaps eventually by planting new congregations, or assisting existing ones.

As a church, we have tried to become more sensitive to others who join with us, whether they are Christians or not, and more concerned for the thousands in our city who have no knowledge of Christ. We are more flexible, more open to new ideas, and I hope we are becoming more authentic and real in our discipleship. We believe in every member having a role in the total ministry of the church and are thrilled to see so many more playing their part in the different aspects of our life together. But we have a long, long way to go. Anything that is being accomplished of lasting value is due to God's grace alone and is to his glory alone. 'The Day will bring it to light. It will be revealed with fire, and the fire will test the quality of each man's work' (1 Cor. 3:13).

What we are building of the character of Christ in our personal and corporate lives is what matters most. Our outreach to others must be the overflow of Christ's life within us, or it cannot be lastingly effective. Our growth in Christ-likeness will be the greatest contribution any of us ever make to the evangelisation of our generation. So, we give thanks for what God has just begun to do and pray that none of us will hinder his purposes. For 'he is able to do immeasurably more than all we ask or imagine, according to his power that is at work within us' (Eph. 3:20).

Chapter 5

Townhead Church, Coatbridge

Peter Bisset

Townhead Parish Church (Church of Scotland) is situated in a postwar housing development at Coatbridge in Lanarkshire. It has experienced considerable growth over the past few years and has an average congregation on a Sunday of about 250 people. Its total membership now stands at around 550.

The minister, the Rev. Charles A. Leggat, was born in Glasgow in 1938. Prior to studying for the ministry he was a shipping clerk. In 1979 he obtained a B.D. from Glasgow University, and in 1980 a Certificate in Pastoral Studies from Edinburgh University. He is married, with six children, and he gives his main interests as his family, and sport.

The Rev. Peter Bisset, M.A., B.D., author of this chapter, was educated at Rutherglen, near Glasgow, and at Glasgow University. For the past ten years he has been warden of St Ninian's Training and Resource Centre for mission and renewal in Crieff, Perthshire. He is married, with three children, all of whom are now married, and his main leisure interests are music, reading and walking.

The young man working on the church roof replacing missing slates was viewed with some apprehension by the Session Clerk of the congregation who looked on from a safe distance. He was grateful for the young man's enthusiastic eagerness to give practical service to the kirk. He was equally glad to see a relatively costly repair being carried out at no charge to church funds. His only anxiety was that the young man's enthusiasm might be greater than his skill! The young man had, however, an experience and expertise beyond the Session Clerk's imagining. His voice sounded out from the heights of the church roof, addressing his distant spectator. 'Harry,' he said, 'seven years ago I was up here pinching the lead!'

The anecdote illustrates something of the remarkable story of Townhead Church, Coatbridge, where over the past three years membership has increased by forty-nine per cent from a recorded total of 343 at the outset of 1981 to a communicant roll of 510 at the end of 1983.

The survivors

Coatbridge is an industrial town at the heart of central Scotland. It is an area particularly associated with coal and steel and has suffered from the decline in these industries. The town itself is at first sight a typical urban disaster area. The centre has been torn out by commercial development and the process appears to have created a wasteland in the midst of the old town. With an unemployment rate in the area of approximately twenty-five per cent, the dull greyness of urban deprivation hangs heavy over the community.

For all of this there is something about the town which the casual observer might not see – the sturdy loyalty of working people who have passed through hard times and through these hard times have learned the dogged persistence of 'survivors'.

Perhaps it was that spirit which alone ensured the survival of Townhead Church over a long period of difficult years. The area which gives the church its name is a post-war housing scheme with a population of approximately 6,500, of which sixty per cent is Roman Catholic. The high percentage of Roman Catholics bears witness to the largely working-class nature of the community and the strong Irish Catholic influence in an area which has experienced successive waves of immigration since the late eighteenth century, as Irishmen came to work as labourers in the heavy industries, bringing with them the religious differences of their own divided land. The result of this is, of course, a community which has developed strongly partisan loyalties, and a large degree of sectarian bitterness.

It was not the most promising location for a new congregation but the Church of Scotland accepted the obligation to serve the community as the National Church and planted a congregation in the area in 1950, building a church to serve the new parish in 1954.

It was a favourable time for church extension. The founding of the new church in Townhead was part of a significant endeavour to plant congregations of the Kirk in all the new housing areas which were springing up throughout the land. Indeed, a report to the General Assembly of that period reflects with a real degree of euphoria what was being experienced in the new housing areas.

> . . . the rebirth of the church as a vital organism conscious of its weakness but vibrant with zeal to extend Christ's Kingdom among men. If church extension is not an expression of the impulse of mission within the church it is nothing at all. Without buildings of substance or tradition the church in the new communities has had to start again with nothing to offer men and women but the Gospel and in the open air and crowded living-rooms and school class-rooms and contractors' huts, in all kinds of so called 'secular' surroundings, the Gospel has been declared with a new simplicity and directness. It is also worthy of note that most of the significant experiences of evangelism at the present time have either originated or been re-moulded in the crucible of church extension endeavour, visitation campaigns, house churches, 'Tell Scotland' groups, adult religious training, the ministry of intercession for the sick, and concern with the whole life of the community.

The writer's account may be euphoric but it was so with good reason. These were stirring days in the land. A missionary movement headed up by Scotland's noted Evangelical leader, Tom Allan, under the banner 'Tell Scotland', sought to mobilise congregations throughout the land in mission. It was clearly seen and proclaimed that the advance of the Church's mission must be through the local congregation making effective witness. Within that witness the role of the laity was seen as decisive.

From 1947 to 1956 the Kirk in Scotland advanced. When Billy Graham responded to the invitation of 'Tell Scotland' to lead the 'All Scotland Crusade' in that year it appeared that the advance of the Kirk was unstoppable. Over the decade from 1946 to 1956 membership increased by five per cent. The tragedy was that over the next eight years all these gains were lost and a pattern of decline established which has not ceased since.

In Townhead it appeared that the story of the church at large would not be reproduced. The momentum of growth was sustained until in 1962 the membership roll recorded a peak of 927 members. From that point onwards, however, it was downhill all the way until in 1980 a new ministry began with the induction of a new minister, the Rev. Charles Leggat.

The new minister did not find a promising situation. The congregation numbered 334 and there had been doubt whether the local Presbytery, which had to judge upon the matter, would allow another ministry. On the face of it it did not appear that this small community could sustain a separate congregation. The bulk of the population was served by the local Roman Catholic Church. It did not appear that the Protestant minority was sufficiently sizeable to make a separate congregation viable. Common sense would have ordained that this small struggling congregation should be linked with some other charge to allow scope for a new ministry. That might have seemed the logic of the situation, but the congregation at Townhead fought hard for survival and a new ministry was granted.

A new beginning: a leader at one with his people

The new ministry had a significant beginning. When Charlie Leggat first came to see the parish he knew that for him it was the place of God's calling. From that point on the process of being 'heard', 'elected' and 'called' was simply a necessary procedure to be followed as God's unfolding purpose was fulfilled.

From the congregation's standpoint the new ministry was

no less happy an arrangement. Charlie belonged. He was one of them. A late entrant to the ministry, he had no pretensions to being anything other than a working man. Before training for the ministry he had worked as a clerk in Glasgow and Grangemouth shipping offices, going to and fro from office to docks, checking the freight of the cargo boats which came to berth. He knew the world, the everyday world of working men, sharing their hopes, their longings and their fears. Settling in the community with his wife and six children it was as though in God's design he had been specially prepared both for such a place as this and such a time as this.

For the Kirk Session there was certainly a deep sense that this was so. Their new pastor was a man of God whom they increasingly grew to love and respect. He was a man like themselves. He understood all the longings and frustrations and the deep sense of hurt and failure which they had experienced through these years of decline. He appreciated the deep instincts which had made them fight for survival.

Harry Towers, Session Clerk at this period, recalls the mood of the time when he records the unhappiness of a Kirk Session which saw little hope for the future and felt that all their endeavours were part of an unremitting struggle for survival. They were at rock bottom and they knew it. Impatience ruled the stormy meetings of Session. Problems of finance dominated their agenda. Fellowship was nil and strangely enough, Harry records, during these days the Word was being proclaimed but its message was unheard.

A personal pentecost

And then there came a new day in their experience. Under Charlie's kindly guiding they began to see a need within their own ranks for renewal and fellowship. It was at that point that as Warden of St Ninian's Crieff (the Church of Scotland Centre for Mission and Renewal) I first encountered the folk from Townhead. There was a marvellous straightforward honesty about them. They had come on a quest. They meant business and their business was with their Lord.

Not surprisingly the Father saw their need, heard their

prayer and answered their longing, and that weekend
Pentecost became a reality in their experience. It was the
church treasurer, who as a member of the group, declared at
the outset the desire which was deep in his heart. 'I need to
be a new man,' he said. At Sunday lunch when all the guests
were packed in a crowded dining-room he stood to his feet to
tell everyone what had happened in his experience. 'I *am* a
new man,' he said.

A minister of the Church of Central Africa Presbyterian,
resident at St Ninian's at that time, sensed most surely what
was happening. 'It is the Holy Spirit,' he said. The sounds of
praise in St Ninian's confirmed that fact. The overflowing
love shown for each other at the final Communion service
heralded for the elders from Townhead the beginning of a
new day.

It was so when they returned home. One wife phoned
another to ask the question, 'Has it happened to your man
too?' A wondering teenager asked of his mother, 'What's
happened to Dad? He's different.' Word spread speedily
through the congregation. The wonderment grew. These
men were 'radiant'.

At the Kirk Session the difference was apparent. Gone, for
the moment at least, were the years of frustrated bickering
and strife. The unresolvable problems were resolved. A new
depth of fellowship brought a new quality of discussion and a
new clarity of vision. From an inward-looking church they
became an outward-looking church. The consequences of
the new ministry and the new unity within the church's
leadership were almost immediately apparent. Townhead
had left behind them almost two decades of decline.
Membership in the first year of the new ministry increased
by twenty-nine per cent and prompted a wondering enquiry
from the Presbytery Clerk to ensure that no error had been
made in the annual statistical return which for so long had
recorded the unremitting downwards plunge. Significantly
enough, with a congregation which has now risen to a
membership of 550, Sunday attendance is of the order of
250. This would be above the normal average attendance at
Sunday worship in the Church of Scotland, but even more
significantly this attendance level is judged by office-bearers
to exceed the attendance twenty years ago when the church

had a membership roll of over 900. It is a special joy to Charlie that the evening service, which is a distant memory in many Scottish kirks, normally attracts a congregation of 60 to 100.

Realising the local leadership potential

It is not surprising, however, that Charlie, who shares his ministry extensively with his elders, rejoices most of all that some of these men who were shy and retiring people have found a new confidence in Christ, which is enabling them to lead the home groups which are assuming an important place in the church's life. The fact that these groups now outnumber the attendance at the Minister's Bible Study and Prayer Group gives Charlie rich encouragement.

Perhaps that facet of the story of Townhead makes it outstandingly encouraging for anyone who looks for pointers for church growth. The parish does not provide a model based on suburban success, or suggest ways of 'winning' which are significantly dependent upon outstanding gifts of pulpit eloquence, or entrepreneurial brilliance. Charlie is a man of God and a man of the people, a humble man who looks rather wonderingly at all that has happened, gives thanks to God but is persuaded with difficulty that there is anything terribly outstanding about his ministry. He will talk more freely about the men and women whom God has given him – the ordinary folk with whom he would number himself, whom he sees as his partners in the enterprise of the gospel.

The evidence of that was apparent when Charlie took ill with a worsening heart condition which necessitated major surgery and six months' absence from the parish. The work of the ministry in Townhead was effectively carried forward by the elders who pastorally and in pulpit ministry kept the church on course. A bonus was presented to Charlie on his return to duty when it was announced that his office-bearers in his absence had decided to build a new, more convenient manse for their minister. It was a far cry from the old days of struggle and frustration.

It is the stories of people in Townhead which, however,

perhaps best tell the story and give pointers towards the secrets of the church's growth.

Changed lives

Billy was, until he lately moved home, an elder in Townhead. A product of the Glasgow slums, he learnt early the ways of petty crime, and the arts of survival in a rough, tough world. It was, however, violence which held the greatest attraction for him. As a boy he had discovered the satisfaction he found in the sight of blood, and remembers vividly having to be dragged away from another boy to whom he had given a savage beating. As the years went by he learned the arts of karate, started carrying a bayonet and developed a strange consuming desire to kill.

All this was aided by ten months spent in London where he found employment after being made redundant. His family now stayed in the city and he found himself back within an environment where all evil seemed to flourish.

One associate was a drug addict, attending a mental hospital and feeding his tortured mind on the perversions of horror literature. Billy was given his introduction to that twisted world. Such religious belief as he had was at that point deserted. He felt that God had forgotten and abandoned him. His response was to ridicule all things Christian. Jesus was a drunk who had died simply because he was a coward and wouldn't stand up to the Romans. And if Jesus was less than a man, God was a failure if he couldn't do anything about it. Christians, of course, only followed their leader and were a weak-kneed bunch who unbelievably chose to go to church and listen to the sermons of boring ignorant ministers.

Billy belonged to the real world of drug pushers and professional heavies and boasted of his association with a fraternity of junkies, con men, alcoholics and rogues. Well nigh incredibly there was, however, another side to the story. In the midst of it all Billy met and married Carole who, though not a church member, at least had had an upbringing in the Kirk. They had a church wedding and were blissfully happy. Two girls were born and in his home Billy found a real place of calm amidst the confusion of his mind.

Apart from his family, he felt the whole world was his enemy and above all blamed this 'daft God character' for his tormented soul. At home no one would have believed what was going on in Billy's heart. The desire to kill, the paranoid lust for power, the hidden desire to trade his soul to the devil was expressed in the simple act of spitting at the church each time he passed by

He felt that he was walking down a cold dark tunnel. But surprisingly there were areas of warmth which were beginning to penetrate the dark cold hardness of his inner being. He had made new friends who were Christians, and though he despised what he had come to see as weakness, he had to acknowledge that they had found a way of love and peace to which he was a stranger.

And then there was Tracy, his daughter. Tracy was almost five. She went to the local playgroup, where the leader was a Sunday School teacher at the parish church. She told the children about Sunday School and awakened the interest of Tracy at least.

Passing by the church with her Dad one day, Tracy, with all a child's innocence, enquired 'Is that God's house, Daddy?' 'Does Jesus live there?' 'Does Jesus love me?' Billy gave easy answers to her childish prattle until the insistent logic of the child drove him to dumbness. Asked Tracy, 'Why don't you let me go?'

There was something else happening which was forcing Billy to think about the faith he had long rejected. Another child was born. With marvellous appropriateness he was given the name 'Christopher'. But old yearnings were wakening in the breast of Billy's wife, Carole. She wanted her children 'christened'.

So far as Billy was concerned it was a case of anything for a quiet life. He loved his wife dearly and recent events with their neighbours had caused real hurt to Carole who knew little of the driving demons in Billy's heart. It had all started with a complaint regarding the behaviour of their neighbour's son. But for Billy the incident unleashed the devil of violence within. Hospital and worse were his promise to the neighbour who wisely retreated to the safety of his home. Carole was justly scared.

The children's baptism was small price to pay for domestic

peace. The only problem was that 'christening' was not quite so easy to arrange as Billy had imagined. The ways of the Kirk were strange, and Kirk law incomprehensible.

It might all have come to a halt at that point for Billy if it had not been for a neighbour. She came to visit them and asked if they were having the baby christened. That might in itself have been yet another dead end if she had not along with her enquiry volunteered to take Billy to meet the minister.

Billy recalls the strong urge within him which made him agree, but beyond that urge there was an assurance born of the word that was passing round the district of a new minister in Townhead, a man with the love of Christ in his heart.

There are two people who specially remember that night when the neighbour took Billy to meet the minister at Townhead church. Tracy accompanied her Dad and was very excited to be in God's house. Billy recalls meeting Charlie, the firm warmth of his handshake, the welcome of Christian love, and the strange sense within his own heart that somehow it was being purged of the spirit of hate.

Everything else flowed from that night: his introduction to the church, the welcome he received from the people he had condemned, the knowledge of the love of Jesus which flooded his heart with peace and joy. Billy and his family came into church membership and Billy still witnesses to the love of Christ made real to them in the fellowship of his church. Today Billy is an elder of the Kirk and rejoices in the wonder of all that God has done.

Lessons learned

Townhead knows from its previous experience the story of growth and decline. There is little doubt that the congregation presently is rejoicing in the surge of new life and vitality which has carried them forward into a new experience of hopefulness. They are, however, aware that the rocket-like advance, following upon the years of decline, is but the beginning of a 'lift off' which must now be sustained with new vision, sure endeavour, and openness to what God wills for them as his people.

There are, however, significant features of their experience upon which they appreciate their continued advance must surely depend.

Firstly, they know from their experience that growth is a sign of life, the outward evidence of the inward renewing of the Spirit of God. They know that their growth began with the transforming experience of the Spirit's power and they know that the way ahead must be one of continued openness to his direction and control.

Secondly, they know that the Spirit is a Spirit of love, and they rejoice in the fellowship that has been born in the love of Christ made real in their experience. They are aware that as the congregation grows it will be most likely in the house fellowships that the love in Christ will be most evidently known.

Thirdly, they know the Spirit as a Spirit of power who has revealed himself in the stories of changed lives. They know that their continuing advance will be not only as the 'old, old story' is retold from their pulpit, but as new stories begin in the lives of the people in their parish.

Fourthly, they know that the Spirit gives his people gifts for service and they have seen this particularly in the gifts of leadership given to ordinary folk who have led the church's advance. Their leadership team is now at the point where it must grow and there is much prayer in Townhead that God will raise up his own people for leadership to carry the congregation forward to new dimensions of growth.

Chapter 6

Community Church in Tottenham, Waltham Forest and Ilford

Dave Halls

This recently established fellowship, with three separate catchment areas in urban and suburban parts of north-east London, has an attendance on an average Sunday of 400, with a communicating membership of about 325. It is led by a team: John Singleton is the senior pastor, and he is supported by Loxley Ford and Dave Halls, author of this chapter, and by four other elders.

Dave Halls was born in 1949 to Pentecostal parents and brought up on a council housing estate in Dagenham. After studying Social Administration at Birmingham University he went into teaching, specialising in remedial work, for three years, and then moved to Bible Society, where he became Scripture Development Manager.

He is married to Wendy, and they have four children. He lists his hobbies as reading, travel, watching TV and doing up an Edwardian terraced house.

'Community Church in Tottenham, Waltham Forest and Ilford' is not the easiest name to live with but it does suit a church with three congregations, stretching along the north-eastern fringe of Greater London. Even describing our catchment area is less than straightforward. When Greater London was reorganised, almost twenty years ago, all the names were changed but even those of us who were children when it all happened still feel part of the old towns; like

Tottenham, in the London Borough of Harringey, or Ilford, in the London Borough of Redbridge.

But be that as it may, there are some things that go on for ever, like the A406 (the North Circular for most of its route) which links our three congregations as it skirts the capital from west to east. At its northernmost point it touches Tottenham, moving east through Waltham Forest until it comes to an end at Ilford.

Constituent congregations

The three congregations are by no means next-door neighbours, with three miles between Tottenham and Waltham Forest and another four to central Ilford. However, if you keep out of the rush hour, Tottenham and Ilford are well under half an hour's travelling time apart. Within each congregation the membership is reasonably concentrated. If you were to draw a one-mile circle from a central point in each case you would enclose fifty to seventy per cent of the members.

Differences between the areas are, to some extent, reflected in the make-up of the congregations. Tottenham has a large, though declining, privately rented housing sector. Our congregation there is just over a hundred, of which single young people, in their twenties and living away from home, account for thirty-five. There are ten Afro-Caribbeans and six Cypriots in the congregation, a somewhat smaller proportion than in the host population.

The part of Waltham Forest where our congregation concentrates is quite different; suburban with higher-priced houses. A significant proportion of this, the smallest congregation, is families with children. It has the highest average age. The largest of the congregations, in Ilford, has about 150 adults. The membership is demographically mixed with two foci, one on the Becontree estate, a between-the-wars, local authority housing development, and the other on a crumbling Edwardian housing estate, mostly owner-occupied, close by.

Overall our 325 adult members are considerably younger than the general London population. Hardly any of us are over fifty years old. It is slightly higher in social class, measured by occupation, and considerably higher qualified. Only five per cent of the church are of Afro-Caribbean origin and there are just two Asians.

Church meetings are held in school halls on Sunday mornings and occasional weeknight events use local church halls. (Our only premises are a small hall and office on the fringe of the area.) Once a month the three congregations meet together, just off the North Circular, for celebration. Putting a meeting together for 500 people in an empty school hall is no small task. With a fifteen-piece band and a portable stage, sound rig, seats and children's meetings to sort out, a lot of people are fully involved. In the summer we eat lunch together and hire the school swimming pool which gives a focus for older children and a ready opportunity for baptisms. Just recently, with an increase in the number of new Christians, baptisms have moved to the local congregations. (It makes more sense that way.)

To a large extent each of the congregations has a life of its own. Each meets in a school hall on Sunday mornings and has its own network of small groups and a distinct framework for pastoral care. We involve as many as possible in pastoral care, stressing mutual responsibility and trying to avoid centring everything around a paternalistic home group leader. Meetings for prayer, outreach and social events are locally organised. Each congregation has a leadership team responsible for local meetings, first line pastoral oversight, evangelism and organisation.

Among centrally organised activities are a rock band and choir. In fact, most musical activity gains strength from cross-church planning. Youth work is centrally co-ordinated and we have singles groups for eighteen- to thirty-year-olds and thirty- to fifty-year-olds.

Leadership and management styles

The church is held together by a team of elders, who share responsibility for the whole church. John Singleton, the senior pastor, (a title we don't actually use) and two others make up a management group, with particular cross-church functions. Four of the elders are full-time, as is the church administrator. None of the full-time staff is theologically trained but all the management group have management experience. Each of the elders is involved in at least one of the local teams but has a considerable role in the spiritual guidance of the whole church.

For now we have an eldership team of seven. Four of the elders have only recently been recognised. Their names were put forward by existing elders; local leadership teams were consulted and the people in the church were asked to respond. Most were enthusiastic. When pressed, few felt the need to make a positive response, fewer still had doubts or queries and even then most of these were 'technical' rather than 'personal'. That could be because we have a highly dependent deferential membership. But a more likely explanation for the lack of response was that the new elders had emerged within local leadership teams and had been functioning at a level where eventual recognition seemed a matter of course.

The relationship between management group and the rest of the elders is, for the present, an easy one. The church does not revolve around one charismatic preacher/leader. Even John, as undoubtedly key leader, has developed with the church rather than being obviously in the forefront from the start. As it is, his basic gift is in government/leadership; public ministry is subsidiary and his most obvious central role is taking the lead in both management group and eldership. His is more than a chairmanship role but far less than autocratic headship.

Our goal is to emphasise the role of groups in leadership rather than individuals, recognising important differences between elders, for instance, but strongly emphasising the corporate nature of their leadership. Not every elder gets to take part in all decisions (although each has the right to speak and to know what is going on). That is inevitable as the church grows. In any case, we wish to share the leadership with others outside the eldership at every possible point, partly as a principle and partly as a training exercise against the day when the congregations become separate churches.

We expect that as local growth occurs and leadership skills develop, the congregations will become churches in their own right, though even on our most optimistic projections, we find it difficult to imagine any size at which occasional

Sunday morning central celebration would be inappropriate. The present level of devolution seems to meet the needs of most people inside the church. Consequently, we are determined to develop local visibility in a way which isn't dependent on the Sunday morning services being in the same place every time. It seems quite unreasonable to be forced into buying a building for such a reason.

Relating to the wider house church context

In the early seventies, house churches sprang up all over the country, and north-east London was no exception. As escapees from the mainstream evangelical churches, mostly in our early twenties, we had been unable to come to terms with restrictions placed on worship and the use of our new-found 'charismatic' gifts. In addition, our radical attitudes to church structure had been an irritant to complacent church life and in desperation, the most vociferous of us had been told by our parent churches, 'Conform or else!' By no means every time was it the charismatic issue. A significant proportion of the founder members of our church were ex-Pentecostals.

We tended to cluster around one or more slightly older figures who were a source of wise advice and at times, clear direction. As is the way with things, these clusters and their leaders were very much aware of marginal differences between themselves and by 1976 there were quite distinct networks extending across the country. Our local network, part of an increasingly nationwide link-up, was drawn together by its foundational ministries with a view to becoming one church.

While most of the constituent groups had grown rapidly in their first year or two, a plateau had been quickly reached. None had more than forty adults, some were as small as fifteen. Each had a leadership ability without the necessary broad base to sustain growth. We lacked other resources too – the ability to arrange large celebrations or fund full-time ministry. And young couples were rapidly becoming parents and needing programmes for their children.

During 1977, monthly Saturday night celebrations and Sunday morning meetings provided an alternative to the small group house meeting. Alongside them frequent meetings with meals, visiting speakers and much discussion provided a forum for integrating local leaders.

In February 1978 regular Sunday meetings commenced with 110 people. The new church was on the way. By the end of the year a series of teaching sessions was convened for the 200 potential members of the new church and on their conclusion most of the people indicated their commitment by signing their name on a slip of paper and dropping it into a grocery carton by the door.

Probably, most of us wish that we had arrived where we are today by a different route. But it would be difficult to imagine what that could have been. Without the networks, we would have had little chance of getting together. Without the strength of the outside ministries our insecurities would have kept us small and isolated.

By 1981, the church had reached its first major crossroads, steered to that point by the men who had originally got it on the road. It was widely agreed that a stronger pastoral orientation was called for, requiring a different balance of leadership. Growth had been fast: to 320 members in January 1981, mainly through transfer from other, more or less local, churches.

A new leadership, under the supervision of the old, began a process of rationalisation. Cohesiveness was lacking, at least on the fringes. Some people had been travelling unrealistic distances, from as far as Ealing in west London, and even the north and east Londoners found the weekly trek to a school hall in Walthamstow unsatisfying.

Happily it was possible to find another church on the edge of west London for the Ealingites. They were sent off happily with their new pastor participating in the farewell event. There was a growing group from Loughton on the borders of Essex, too, who were 'planted out' with their own leaders. Loughton isn't so far away, but it's not quite Greater London. That trimmed the church by around forty members.

But cohesiveness was affected by other factors. A considerable number of the apparently committed members had carried doubts all the way along and had been less than enthusiastic even though they had signed their names. They really wanted to be part of something quite different – smaller, far more local, with less attention being given to objectives and growth.

Our travelling ministries advised a thorough sort out. When the basis of commitment was spelled out again, around fifty decided not to opt in. That was traumatic enough, with the implied criticism on both sides. (It is worth noting that after three years apart we are good friends again.) But during the summer an impasse was reached between the local leadership and the outside ministries, who held the final authority in the church, leading to a fundamental break. The detail doesn't really matter. We felt that the specifics of outside control threatened the integrity of the local church. They felt we were rebellious. What made the stress of parting far worse was that, as local leaders, we had believed that external authority was essential for our very survival. That we were acting in the light of conviction seemed little consolation.

A dreadful doom was foretold but, by our standard at least, it never arrived. Changes in the way we do things, and in particular in our relationships with other churches, have been far greater than we could have ever imagined. Inevitably, without what had become a countrywide network, transfer growth was less likely. We had lost visibility and our strongly promoted recruitment drive was past whether we liked it or not.

With clearer minds and our commitment to growth intact, we focused on evangelism. A long-standing suspicion was confirmed. Lots of Anglican churches were seeing a higher percentage of conversions than us. We needed to learn; not to teach. And learn we have. Growth is still a painful process. If people want to join us from other churches we let them. But we don't go out of our way to attract people who are happily settled.

From 1978 to mid 1981, local transfer accounted for eighty per cent of all growth. The effect on relationships with other local churches is easily imagined. Over the last two and a half years that proportion has dropped to forty per cent. As we have tried to work with other churches, as allies rather than as competitors, we have made a lot of friends who are providing important support. In some places things are still prickly but we do what we can to find healing and demonstrate our change of heart.

Soon after the changes of 1981, one of our leaders telephoned an old acquaintance, a pastor in another house church stream, to arrange lunch. While talking he felt it necessary to explain, 'Look, I don't want to sound over the top but we really would like to see you – we haven't got any hidden motive – we'd just like to see you.' To his surprise his acquaintance sounded relieved. 'I needed to hear that,' he replied. The approach which we had typified, of wanting to own everything we could and dismiss everything we couldn't had resulted in people wondering what new scheme we were hatching even when we telephoned to fix a lunch appointment.

That pastor is now part of a fraternal in which two of our elders are involved. Like others with which we are involved, the fraternal is becoming increasingly important in clarifying vision, building relationships and acting together.

From the beginning of 1981 we had planned for the emergence of three distinct congregations. As a result we needed a change of name. North London Community Church, our original name, made little sense in east London. We are still N.L.C.C. for official purposes, but our newer, longer title is central to our corporate image. (The local congregations are known as Community Church in Tottenham, or Ilford etc.)

So 1981 was clearly a watershed. From that time we have had a more relaxed attitude to membership, though we are still aware that a high level of commitment from a high proportion of people is essential in making a church like ours work. We have been free to drink at many streams; seeking advice from leaders in older churches as well as new, and making more friends than we have lost.

Evangelism: from lip-service to lifestyle

The most significant change has been that we have moved from paying lip-service to evangelism to trying to make it part of our lifestyle. The years 1978–81 saw considerable growth. Churches have only a certain amount of energy to expend and attention to give to new people. Ours went to local transfers. Less than five per cent of the 200 who joined us in that period were new Christians. During 1982 and 1983 just over 100 new people have become involved, of whom forty were new converts and forty local transfers. The rest have moved into the area.

Almost all our new Christians come to Christ through their friends. Doug had been converted after buying himself out of the army at the age of twenty. His friends were part of a church in Coventry and as Doug lived in London, they put him in touch with us. Vic, his school-friend turned drinking partner, was encouraged to see Doug's new housegroup. He came with two problems. His knee was painful from a sports injury, and he and his young wife, Winnie, did not get on.

The housegroup prayed for his knee and his salvation at the same time. Vic experienced some healing following the laying on of hands and was saved, more or less simultaneously. This was around the summer of 1981 when the three congregations had just been formed, and the concerted attention of the Ilford people was brought to bear on Winnie. She and Vic had been wanting a baby, and once the church knew she was pregnant, after several years of hoping, they were confident she too would soon be a Christian. Winnie started to visit Vic's new circle. She was befriended by a variety of young mums in the congregation and in the event the baby was born just after she was born again.

This all happened as we were beginning to feel our way in evangelism. Winnie was a sort of first-fruits. They were living several miles away from any of our main concentrations of membership and as soon as they could afford it they moved house to be closer. Just recently they led their new next-door neighbours to the Lord, another young couple with two small children.

Nothing like the whole church is as yet mobilised in evangelism but there are many other cases of contact evangelism. Dorette talked to the man who repaired her telephone and he came to a meeting. Mike and his wife fed Derek, the student in the flat downstairs. Cheryl spoke to Clare at school, who brought her mum. She talks to everyone; friends, workmates, relations, neighbours.

The exact steps by which each person has come to Christ

are not easy to untangle. In some cases the light was switched on suddenly, in others it dawned slowly. In most cases the commitment was made outside a meeting; in personal conversation, perhaps with the initial contact, or in a small group.

It is rarely possible to put somebody into a new Christians' group immediately but we do try to stay close, build friendships and as soon as possible talk about baptism and receiving the Holy Spirit.

Problems of integrating new believers

It is easy to assume, in churches like ours, that the integration of new believers and transfers alike is straightforward. The apparent informality of large events, the many small groups, the use of neutral buildings for meetings, should all make joining gentle and unstressful. That is far from the case.

The problem is less for transfers, particularly those who have already made up their minds to join us. Most will have friends in the church already. It has to be accepted that few people are likely to drift into a church without a worship centre. With so few who arrive that way, we have developed no programme for the Christian fringe. Hardly any half-way-house activities exist and the weekday programme, relying as it does on lifestyle involvement, small groups and task activities, is difficult to mesh into unless you are in the know. If you don't know anybody in the church already the outlook is bleak, particularly should you need to spend a long time on the edge of the church making up your mind to get involved. We know we need Welcome Teams. But when casual visitors are such a small proportion of new growth, they are inevitably not our first priority.

During our first four years, newcomers were required to join a Foundation Course, at the end of which they were asked to write to the elders expressing why they wanted to join the church. During this period they were not normally allowed to take part in any church activity other than the Sunday morning meeting, for fear of having people join for wrong reasons. Applicants were interviewed by the elders on the basis of their letter and, if all was satisfactory, they were welcomed into the life of the church.

Now the way we do things is far more relaxed. The end point in the process is still the public welcome and the Welcome Buffet, which has become such a tradition that people would feel shortchanged without it! But immediately they express a desire to join the church, they are encouraged to get involved wherever they can.

At the same time they are invited to join a Foundation Group for a period of between three and six months, where much the same material is used as before, but over a longer period. The emphasis is far more on building relationships and taking part in small group meetings. So by the time they officially join they are already well integrated and have faced up to the issues we consider important for being part of the church.

The content of the course is determined by two workbooks. The first, *Christian Foundations*, covers the life of the believer and his relationship with God – The Love of God, the Cross, Repentance, Faith, Baptism, Christian living.

Over the years we have been encouraged by the number of people who look back to that period of reviewing their Christian experience as important. One girl in her early twenties had been a churchgoer for years but found a personal faith only during the course. A week later she died suddenly, an event which made us realise how important the course could be.

The second workbook, *What am I Letting Myself in For?*, is common to transfers and new Christians alike; it is about being part of a church. We have wondered whether the longer-term Foundation Group has fudged issues for those transferring, which otherwise would have been faced squarely. The evidence at present does not support that view. Previously twenty-five to thirty per cent of those starting Foundation Courses decided not to join the church. When we dispensed with that procedure we thought that, as a result of making it easier to join, people might find themselves trapped into something that they later wished to opt out of. So far this has not been the case. We have never had a very high attrition rate and, if anything, it has declined over the past two years. As for letting in people who are likely to be troublesome, we have the Holy Spirit and our wits to guide us. Formal membership screening offers little protection.

For the new Christian, integrating into church life can be particularly problematic even when introduced by a friend. Our Sunday morning meetings are long: two hours even when tightly disciplined. Initial worship takes three quarters of an hour, longer if it is going well. If we break bread it will take a good half an hour in small groups or possibly informally: moving around the room, praying with one another. Preaching will, at its very minimum, take another forty-five minutes. Probably the lively music, changes in pace and most importantly, the sense of family, balance out the length of the meeting. Prayer for the sick or others in need, prophecy, tongues, dancing, people telling their story, all add to the immediacy for the young and unchurched. For some others it can be a threatening time, necessitating easy-going explanations.

In the small group meetings there are another set of problems. We rarely work through a programme. Most people, for good or ill, prefer to 'let it flow'. For the uninitiated, such a fellowship meeting can be a perturbing experience. Starting off the meeting is done subtly. Old hands will know how to watch out for nonverbal signals from the meeting leader. Chatting away over a hushed silence as the meeting starts, the new person is likely to be acutely embarrassed.

Traps for the unwary are many. There are nonverbal cues for starting and finishing prayer time. Like all evangelical groups, holy mutters and grunts contribute to the atmosphere even more than jargon. We don't like it. We want to change. We even announce the start of meetings. But old habits die hard!

The answer, with an increase in numbers of new Christians joining the church, has been to start New Christians' Groups which are a conscious attempt to provide a half-way house as well as basic instruction. Materials available for such courses are to our mind unsatisfactory. They seem either too wordy or miss the point. We are producing our own which give a strong emphasis to baptism in water and the filling of the Spirit, alongside developing distinctively biblical attitudes to interpersonal relationships. The success of the New Christians' Groups is evidenced by the fact that people seem genuinely disappointed when we bring them to a halt and once we have cracked the problem of materials for these groups we could have a multi-stage introduction to Christian life and doctrine.

While we have found published materials of little use for our kind of converts, we have found great help from the insights of those who have had special concern with working with new Christians in small groups, like John Mallinson and Lyman Coleman. One of many important things we have gleaned has been the balancing of groups, with each new Christian having an 'older brother' at his elbow to talk to and explain things. We are finding that it makes most sense for those pairs to carry on together so that each new Christian makes that particular link person their connection into the pastoral care structure. Using up older brothers and sisters so fast creates a constant training need which we have yet to cope with adequately.

Overseas links

Overseas involvements have been sporadic but are growing. Following the 1980 earthquake in Central Italy, we were involved in sending prefabricated homes and work parties to erect them. Currently, our main involvement is with Guyana on the edge of the Caribbean. Some of our leaders have visited churches there and we have had an extended financial thrust which people have taken to their hearts. Caribbean visitors share in the church, something which is made possible by our friendships there. A relationship which has developed without planning, it has obvious significance in areas like Tottenham with their kinship links into the West Indies and South America. For several years we have been aware of a word from God, 'Pour out the oil.' We are deeply conscious that such resources as we have should be used to bless others. We try to devote a minimum ten per cent of our income to outside projects but are aware that, as with community involvement, our overseas commitments must increase if we are to follow God fully in the longer term.

Administration

With no major investment in property, we avoid a great part of the administrative burden which falls on most churches. However, it is undoubtedly the case that the existence of a physical centre makes it easier to arrange most events. Our rent bill totals £10,000 a year which represents a considerable workload in hall bookings alone.

Without premises, particularly with three congregations, any internal post system is unreliable, so postage is an increasing cost and complications with circulation lists multiply. Petrol costs are high as well. But for now they represent, in money and work, a small premium for the lack of commitment to property.

Our financial administration is handled by a volunteer book keeper, whose workaday experience in financial management gives us real benefits, and a Covenants Secretary, under the guidance of one of the elders. Since June 1983 we have had a full-time administrator whose work is varied and still a little unpredictable. He is assisted by a typist for ten hours a week.

We feel we have a long way to go in administration, although since all of us involved in management of the church have 'administration' somewhere within our gift mix, we may well be overly critical of our own performance.

Early on in the life of the church we attempted to produce a bi-monthly magazine. The print schedule was such that only two-month-old news got included. It was not a success. Now we have regular monthly notice sheets in each area plus a handwritten internal newsletter. We have just discovered a way of producing good quality photocopies of photographs, so will be producing *Fresh Faces*, an occasional booklet with pictures of new people in the church. No doubt we will have another attempt at a magazine in due course.

Address lists in any growing church are a real problem! We just manage to cope by using one member's small business computer and much photocopying.

Avoiding the plateau

In just over two years we have developed regional congregations, changed the system of pastoral care, bought a portable stage, sound system and the trailer to contain it, achieved a major reorientation towards evangelism and doubled the size of the eldership. We have added over a hundred people and lost, through death, mobility and disenchantment less than thirty. One elder has stepped down. At times the stresses of change have been painful to the point of wondering if we could cope with it all. We are left slightly breathless, and grateful to God that he has been masterminding what has been happening for us.

However, we are very much aware that conscious waiting on God and thorough planning are needed if we are not to reach a plateau at our present size. During the next growth phase we will need to see God's power evidently at work among us if we are to make any significant impact on the area where we live.

That is one side of the coin. On the other we have felt able to begin to discuss an eighteen-month plan for change and development, though we find it difficult to think much beyond that in strategic, if not visionary, terms.

Our first priority, and perhaps a strange one, given our background, is to renew our concentration on shared life in neighbourhoods. We are not quite promoting communal living but we do want much more than housegroup meetings which have little relevance to everyday life. Where we are geographically concentrated, the leadership role will be to facilitate being together: doing things together and not relying on the weekly meeting as the only time to pray together or share God's word. In some places it is already happening. But we would like to see real community life more widespread without putting it in the rule book.

Hard on the heels of this emphasis will be a focus on the neighbourhood fringe of friends, neighbours and community involvement. We have seen already that this kind of evangelism works and, even if there were no Great Commission to help fulfil, looking outward is the best way we know of counteracting introversion and stagnation.

Coming up behind will be major changes in

administration and communication hardware. We will need more staff. There is the possibility of switching our whole operation to computer; word processing for materials; better, more responsive address lists; and a cost-centred accounting system to make sure that we stay in control of expenditure. We are trying to put 'shared life concepts' into print so that we do not lose our distinctive flavour as we get bigger. We need to consider video production for teaching, leadership development and internal communication, particularly sharing testimonies between neighbourhoods and congregations.

In 1985 we would like to achieve greater visibility in the areas in which we work and are considering buying our own Community Church Bus. In rural evangelism and urban community work they are already widely used, so there is a fund of expertise to draw on. It would function as a mobile youth centre and video theatre and could be used by all three congregations: a major project involving a lot of money, a lot of people and vision! That summer we hope to spend on mission, in community projects and other kinds of outreach.

By the autumn we would like to plant a group or two back towards Inner London. Some people will need to move house and where active churches exist in the area, a great deal of talking will be needed if we are to avoid feelings of competition.

That is 'Community Church in . . .' from an inside view. We are very aware that we have grown fast and have yet to prove that we will be stable in the long term. We are also aware that we don't have any major charismatic figure at the helm to take things forward by force of personality. But we are overwhelmingly conscious of God helping us to survive and giving us people with a high level of commitment and great energy. Looking at the dangers on one side and the possibilities on the other, we are doing our best to face up to the blunt exhortation that came to us strongly at the start of the year: 'If you do not stand firm in your faith you will not stand at all.'

Chapter 7

St Mary's and St Cuthbert's, Chester-le-Street

Kerry M. Thorpe

The Parish Church of Chester-le-Street in Co. Durham serves a dormitory and market town with a number of outlying ex-mining communities. The church has grown substantially in recent years, by establishing a network of subsidiary congregations around the town (see map, p.128).

The minister, the Rev. Ian D. Bunting, M.A. (Oxon), Th.M. (Princeton, USA) has been Rector of Chester-le-Street since 1978. Prior to his present appointment he was Vicar of St John's, Waterloo, Merseyside and then Director of Pastoral Studies at Cranmer Hall Theological College, Durham. He is married with five children.

The Rev. Kerry M. Thorpe, author of this chapter, was until 1984 Curate at St Mary's and St Cuthbert's. He is now Vicar of St George's, Fatfield, Washington. He spent four years in the horse racing world and three years as a funeral director and embalmer before training at Oak Hill Theological College, where he obtained a B.D. (London). His previous curacy was on Merseyside, and he is married with two children.

Just before ten o'clock on an average Sunday morning in Chester-le-Street, Co. Durham, north-east England, about seven hundred people of all ages will be making their way to worship at the local Anglican church. They will not all be making their way towards the same building, though. While

OUTLINE MAP OF CHESTER-LE-STREET PARISH

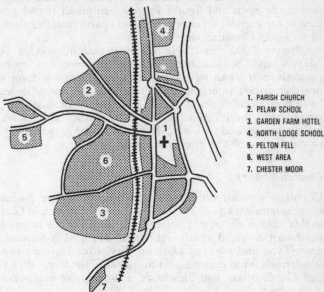

1. PARISH CHURCH
2. PELAW SCHOOL
3. GARDEN FARM HOTEL
4. NORTH LODGE SCHOOL
5. PELTON FELL
6. WEST AREA
7. CHESTER MOOR

Chester-le-Street is just one Anglican parish, with its one church building, the story of growth here is the story of new congregations planted, and growth in diversity.

The present incumbent, Ian Bunting, who became Rector in 1978, describes the pattern of growth like that of the strawberry plant. It is a plant which puts out runners; they take root and growth is extended, encircling the original plant.

Back in the town worshippers will be making their way, some towards the grand old parish church building, some to the assembly halls of local schools, some to a village hall and some to a Tenants Association Social Club. There are now six separate venues for worship under the auspices of the Anglican church on a Sunday morning. There are a further two services at the church building during the day, another two during the week, and one more monthly service in a local community building. On a good week the total can be around a thousand people at worship.

There are, of course, churches of other denominations within the town and figures suggest that about twelve per cent of the population altogether would participate regularly in an act of Christian worship.

Observing the growth in ministry and mission at St Mary's and St Cuthbert's Chester-le-Street has more parallels with watching a test match than with watching a one-day cricket international. That is to say, many issues have been decided slowly; some have turned dramatically; occasionally the outcome has been in doubt. There have been problems and set-backs, decline as well as growth. Even in starting to tell the story it is not obvious where to begin.

Church history

Christian worship on the site of Chester-le-Street parish church dates back to 883 A.D. The story of the work of God in this town is not new. Chester-le-Street lies in the heart of north-east England about eight miles south of Newcastle-upon-Tyne and north of Durham City. Like Durham and Sunderland it has grown up on the banks of the River Wear, and like Durham and Newcastle it lies on the major A1 motorway.

Recorded history of the church starts with the arrival of a Christian community of monks, escaping from Lindisfarne, their Holy Island, after attack. The monks arrived and settled together with the remains of St Cuthbert, their one-time leader and a famed Christian teacher. The fact that the monks settled in Chester-le-Street made it a centre of Christian pilgrimage and worship for the 112 years of their stay. During those years, Chester-le-Street was in fact the cathedral city of the north. Later they moved to Durham and built their cathedral there.

It was, however, in the nineteenth century that the community really developed. With the discovery of coal and the development of mine-workings the population grew fast. The present century has seen continued rapid growth in population, now around 25,000. This century has also seen drastic decline in the coal industry and no working pits now remain within the parish. Chester-le-Street is thus a reflection of the typical history of north-east England.

Painting some of this background is actually quite important for an understanding of the ministry of the parish church. Perhaps fairly unusually for a growing church, St Mary's and St Cuthbert's operates within the traditional Anglican vision of a community church serving the town within a parish structure. There is virtually no eclectic congregation, no drawing of worshippers from other communities. Attempting thus to cater for many approaches to worship, the services range from the chaotically informal to the rigidly traditional. Good relationships exist too between church and town, happily demonstrated in 1983 with joint celebration of 1,100 years of history.

Going for growth

There have been bold attempts in the past to enable the church to fulfil its ministry towards the people of the town. At the end of the nineteenth century, Canon Blunt, then Rector, established mission churches away from the parish church building in the fast-growing outlying communities which had sprung up around the coal pits. None of the pits now survives and the communities themselves have experienced decline. None of the mission churches remains, but today's growth can be seen against the background of this previous visionary endeavour.

Today's story of strawberry-plant growth, of Area Family Service congregations planted around the town, must start with Patrick Blair who was Rector from 1971 to 1977. The vision was Patrick's and so was the pain of first implementing it. His ability to think strategically, to take tough decisions and to live with the consequent unpopularity were God's gift for the moment. A legendary facility for organisation and administration undoubtedly helped too. Patrick Blair inherited a church in which there were deep divisions, much hurt and tension. In the early sixties the parish had reached a peak of regular attendance. Since then it had been a story of steep decline. Patrick came to a shrinking church, and for the early part of his ministry the decline continued. In fact one of the most telling points to emerge in this story is the way in which decline continued well into the early years of the new vision for Area growth.

There must have been times when the evidence suggested that a wrong step had been taken, things appeared worse rather than better, growth seemed a long way off. 'It may seem slow in coming, but wait for it.' God's words to Habakkuk were certainly pertinent here.

Numbers attending the traditional services at the parish church were going down, although the recently started Family Communion service seemed to be meeting a need. The mission churches in the now-declining outlying areas were, except one, defunct. Against this background the vision of a new strategy was born. Clearly, family worship was the one growth point, so some way had to be found of taking the church to where the families were. The church could no longer rely on people commuting in to a building which seemed to hold no relevance for them. Therefore, new Family Service congregations would be planted, this time not in the outlying communities but on the growing estates within the town. These services were to be non-sacramental, and of an informal though structured style. It was hoped that they would be attractive to those hitherto outside the scope of traditional worship and would thus have an evangelistic aim. This was obviously going to involve some degree of local participation in ministry and shared leadership.

First faltering steps

As you might expect, serious reservations about all this were expressed by the Parochial Church Council (P.C.C.), the elected decision-making body within the church. The greatest fears were for parish unity. 'This will destroy the church.' 'We will never recover from this.' Doubts were expressed too over the availability or ability of local lay ministry in preaching, teaching and leading worship.

Despite all this, and in the face of criticism, the first Area Family Service was set up. It was in South Pelaw that the first new plant put down roots, in a housing estate in the north-west of the town. Already a Sunday School existed there, and therefore a base on which to build.

Members of the parish church congregation who lived in Pelaw were asked, by personal invitation of the Rector, to join the new service. Initially, about twenty people formed the core. The first services were held in the Community Hall, and according to one participant they were chaotic! Lay people were asked to lead the service, form and content being laid down by the Rector. Visiting preachers were begged, borrowed or stolen from elsewhere. Even tape-recorded sermons were played to the assembled gathering, not entirely successfully.

Slowly though, the Area Family Service took root. Once a month the Area Service shut down, in favour of a visit to the parish church for Holy Communion. This monthly pattern was to become a feature in all of the Areas, despite the fact that for many the first Sunday became lie-in day rather than Communion day. Part of the reason for this was that for some who had been introduced fresh to the Area Service there was no underlying loyalty to or knowledge of the 'big church' as it became known. More than once the issue of Holy Communion in the Areas has been raised. Outside observers have pointed to its lack as a weakness in the system. However, the symbolism of uniting around the Lord's table at the mother church has seemed worth preserving. Chester-le-Street has consciously refused the already tested path of 'mother and daughter' churches. The formation of new and autonomous parishes within the town has been resisted, preferring instead many branches to the one tree.

Tensions began to emerge within the South Pelaw Area Family Service within its first two years. This was not just between Area Service and parish church, but within the Area congregation itself. The people most closely involved with setting up the new service had come mostly from the Council housing area. Now the service was attracting families from the newer private housing estate. In time much of the local leadership was taken up by those from the other side of the road, the more obviously middle class. Council-house dwellers ceased attending in quite the same numbers, and some returned to the parish church. Although never entirely rectified, the problem was partly resolved when Pelaw were given their own staff member. Ray Hall, Church Army Evangelist, was appointed as full-time overseer of the congregation at South Pelaw in 1974. That was three years after its start, and current members date the stability and real growth of the Service from that point.

Repeating the experiment

Next up the runway was the Garden Farm Area Family Service. Garden Farm was a new estate of owner-occupied houses on the south-west side of town, home for many young families. Before the few willing couples from that area could pioneer this new work, suitable premises had to be found. There really was only one choice – the pub. The Garden Farm Hotel was a modern pub, built along with the estate, and the only available community building. Many were reluctant to leave the safer confines of the parish church to attempt this journey of faith. A small number were willing, and with ministry help from the parish church the service started. Again it was slow going at first. After eighteen months the parish was able to offer accommodation on the estate to an ordained post-graduate student from Durham University, in return for part-time ministry help with the Garden Farm congregation. This system continued with varying degrees of success until the appointment of a full-time Curate in 1978.

In its favour the Garden Farm Area had its abundance of neighbouring young families. It quickly became clear that provision of Sunday School facilities, run in conjunction with the service, was an important key to growth. The need to staff this children's work drew out gifts and commitment from local people. Much of the sense of belonging that helped to establish this service stemmed from that team of Sunday School teachers.

Against it, this area had its slightly less than suitable building. There was a certain amount of novelty value, meeting in the pub. Some came and met with Christ in this setting, people previously put off by the more imposing parish church. Others simply could not make the necessary mental adjustment to see this as a proper church. The practical problems too were quite large. Acoustically, pub lounges do not lend themselves to corporate worship. Aesthetically, meeting alongside the bar was not the most helpful. The Sunday School class met in the Ladies Powder

Room. The sermon was delivered to a congregation assembled around the pool table. Because finishing time for the service and opening time for the pub came fairly close together, the final moments were often accompanied by the clanking of crates and the clinking of bottles.

This Service too ran into problems, people problems, perhaps because of the absence of long-standing tradition, or because of the inevitable tensions of drawing out gifts and giving responsibility. Growth was slow and there were frequent minor squabbles between members. However, some newcomers did find faith in Jesus Christ. Most often the initial openness was due to the provision of a setting for less formal family worship, but still within an Anglican structure. Growth here was almost exclusively amongst those with young children. Nine years on, under the ministry of full-time Curate David Lomas, the congregation had grown to the point at which the pub simply could contain it no longer. By 1981 the average attendance was ninety per week and the building itself inhibited further growth. This time facilities were available and the congregation moved up the hill to the assembly hall at the Hermitage Comprehensive School.

Losses and gains

In 1973, when the first two Area Services were already under way, the last of the old mission churches collapsed. Literally. Pelton Fell, although part of the parish of Chester-le-Street, is in almost all respects a separate little community, lying about two miles out from the town centre. The work in Pelton Fell came into line with the newly developing concept of local mission in community buildings almost by accident. When the building of the mission church had to close, financially there was small prospect of rebuilding. The village hall was well placed, had adequate facilities, and was available. So the transfer of the congregation there was effected.

Pelton Fell has never had the opportunity of its own resident staff member, a lack frequently noted. This need has been partly met over the last few years by the Sunday ministry of Rosemary Nixon, Deaconess and lecturer at

Cranmer Hall in Durham. The smallest of the Area Family Services, Pelton Fell averages an attendance of about thirty people per week. Here, too, some of the tensions noted earlier have been apparent. It has not proved easy integrating newcomers with leadership gifts and more traditional folk with a conservative view of the ministry.

And the next

With three Area Family Services now operative, in addition to the old parish church, people in the north of the town began to get restless. Looking at the ventures in South Pelaw, Pelton Fell and on the Garden Farm Estate, some of the worshippers from the North Lodge area of the town wanted to join the experiment. Early in 1973 Patrick Blair received a petition from North Lodge asking for their own Family Service. John Hall, teacher and Lay Reader, was in turn asked by the Rector if he would head up this new project. In 1974, then, a new venue was added to the list of Area Services, the Secondary School at North Lodge. Once more the informality of the setting and the flexibility of family worship clearly met a need and local families with no previous Christian commitment were drawn in. Interestingly, not many of those who had pressed for the service in the first place stayed to continue the work, many returning in time to the parish church. The pattern that had emerged in the other settings proved true again. Sunday School facilities proved popular, the monthly Communion service down at the parish church did not. Area loyalties seemed to conflict with parish loyalties and the lack of available full-time ministry proved to be a limiting factor. John, as lay reader, found himself increasingly left to fulfil the ministry of leading and teaching. When in 1977 the service had to move out from the main school hall into an unheated prefabricated building, it was one setback too many. During the interregnum after Patrick Blair's departure the North Lodge Family Service was closed down.

Last but not least

Like the tortoise in that well-known fable, there was another area pressing on, making slow but constant progress. The West Area, in sharp contrast to the smart North Lodge end of town, is solidly council-owned property. Deaconess Isabel Wells, when she joined the staff team, was given the task of developing the work in that West Area. Isabel, under Patrick Blair's guidance, set to work visiting and caring pastorally for the people of that neighbourhood. From those already connected with the parish church and those contacted by Isabel, a home-based Bible study group was formed. With that as a start Isabel set up a special mid-week West Area Carol Service at Christmas time. A less adventurous start perhaps, slower and more hesitant than in other areas, but their first Area Service nevertheless. For several years that pattern continued, with other special occasion services being added, Harvest Festival and Mothering Sunday. From there the West Area in 1979 was able to support a monthly family service on a pattern similar to those held elsewhere in the town. Finally by January 1982, ten years on, the West were able to come fully into line with other areas by holding a weekly service. The average attendance was about fifty at this time. Leadership among the local people in this council-house area was not as easy to come by as in other parts. The people felt themselves to be at some disadvantage with the more articulate congregations elsewhere in the church. But with Isabel's caring and sensitive ministry, the existing home-fellowship group became the planning Pilot Group for the new service. In addition, one or two were encouraged to share in the leadership of worship. That process of growth continues.

The venue for West Area services, the Whitehill Park Tenants Association Social Club, like the Garden Farm Hotel earlier, gave rise to some comments – and some raised eyebrows. Coverage in the local press actually helped to raise public awareness of the service. There was an attempt at mischief-making when on one occasion a party, including the appearance of some young female strippers, was booked at the venue to follow on immediately from the Sunday worship. Regular attenders at the service wisely had no comment to make to the press on the matter!

Rebirth of North Lodge

To complete this overview of development in Area Family Services within the parish of Chester-le-Street, we must return to North Lodge. It had by now become clear that two of the key factors, under God, in the success of these ventures were the presence of trained leaders and the availability of a suitable community venue. God answered prayers for both these things and in November 1981 the North Lodge Area Family Service was able to recommence. Rob and Margaret Bianchi joined the parish staff in 1980 from Cranmer Hall, Durham, for a first curacy, Rob as Curate with responsibility for South Pelaw and Margaret as Deaconess allocated to the North Lodge area. Under the direction of the new Rector, Ian Bunting, Margaret met with some of the Christians from that area, now worshipping at the parish church. Together they prayed for God to open a way for the Family Service to restart. As before, accommodation was a problem. The school building was there, the Education authority was agreeable to its use for worship, but it remained firmly locked on a Sunday morning. Some willing person from the school maintenance staff had to be found and the obvious choice, the caretaker, was not prepared to work regularly on Sunday mornings. Prayers were answered, however, when one of the school cleaners offered her services as key bearer. The matter was brought back before the Church Council in October 1981. Having baled out of one venture previously in North Lodge, the Council were understandably wary about starting up again. Doubts were expressed about the ability of the staff, now five full-time, to meet increased demands of ministry in an already busy parish. Again the church faced the obvious call upon local lay ministry, but recognised now more than ever the need to provide adequate support and training for those called to lead and serve. North Lodge was given the go-ahead at the same time as approval was granted for the setting up of a lay-training programme, to equip those called upon to lead and preach in the Areas.

Back at the centre

A word needs to be said here about life back in the parish

church. Over the years 1971 to 1982 four new congregations
had gone out from the centre. What had been the effect of
this constant giving birth? Were there any signs of post-natal
depression? Actually the biggest shock to the system came in
1976. The pattern of worship in the big church had been for
some time like many Anglican churches, that of a weekly
Communion service. In 1976 the Church Council gave
permission for an experimental change. The parish church
would itself now come into line with the new Area Services,
that is, they too would have a weekly non-sacramental family
service and Holy Communion only on the first Sunday in
each month. (Weekly eight a.m. Communion continued
unchanged.) Some worshippers were so unhappy with this
arrangement that they stayed away, boycotting the new
Family Service in the parish church. After the six months of
experimentation a parish-wide referendum was held.
Members of each congregation were asked their opinion.
Was it right for this new pattern to continue, whereby the
main church building would house a weekly non-
sacramental Family service, the same as the Areas? Should
all join together around the Lord's table just once a month?

It was a close-run contest. The opinion of regular parish
church attenders was almost equally divided between
preference for the new system and the old weekly
Communion pattern. The story was different in the Area
congregations, though. They voted overwhelmingly sixty-
eight per cent in favour of the new programme. On the
strength of that vote the decision was taken. The parish
church would toe the line with the Areas. Those worshipping
in the outlying services were thereby being allowed a decisive
voice in the affairs of the old mother church. In turn it was
thus a vote of confidence in the Areas. Perhaps it was a sign
of their coming of age, certainly an affirmation of their place
within the total structure and vision of the parish as a whole.

The Family Service at the parish church has continued to
grow. Average attendance in 1982 was 268. Often, the
merely curious will turn up first at the parish church for a
Sunday service and then perhaps seek out the local
congregation within their own area. There has been
something of a turnover of attenders also and perhaps the
parish church has found it harder than other areas to

integrate newcomers. This problem has been partly offset by Basic Christianity courses run in conjunction with the morning service.

Small-group growth

Under the most recent ministry of Ian Bunting and his wife Mair, small groups have played a major part in bringing newcomers to a faith in Jesus Christ. One of the acknowledged results of Family Service ministry generally is an increase in attendance, not always matched by a similar increase in the number of committed Christians. Family Service ministry can be something of a spectator sport.

Both Ian and Mair have gifts in respect of small-group evangelism. Not long after their arrival, cell groups were sprouting around the town. The Basic Christianity course was perhaps the most usual format initially. Individuals with little or no faith in Christ, those with a vague interest and some longing to know more, were invited along. The course was designed to last eight weeks, and met in the homes of group members. In this setting the claims of Christ were explored and the challenge to personal faith presented. One participant, John, tells of the smokescreen of irrelevant questions that he put up, week by week, anything to keep at bay the growing uncomfortable awareness that God was calling him to a personal response of faith. No figures exist to tell just how many have come into the kingdom through this means, but certainly the count runs into scores. From those initial faith-seeking groups, continuing home-based fellowship groups emerged. The current total of housegroups within the parish is about 23, but it is still not easy to keep accurate figures! The Basic Christianity course format is used now in most of the Areas. At the parish church this course continues, lay-led, week by week as a withdrawal class from the main service. At the appropriate point, adults are able to leave for their course at the same time as children depart for Sunday School classes, with the regular adult worshippers remaining in church for the sermon.

Homing in

Now let us look in a little more depth at just one of the Area

Family Services. When I joined the staff team in Chester-le-Street, in the summer of 1981, it was to take responsibility for the Garden Farm Area. Five months previously the congregation there had negotiated their move from the pub to the Comprehensive School. Average Sunday attendance, including the smallest of children, was ninety. Affairs of the Area Service were administered by a Pilot Group, elected from within the congregation. This group, as in all the Areas, has a lay-chairperson, about ten members and two representatives on the Parochial Church Council. It is responsible ultimately to that P.C.C. Financial affairs are for the most part administered from the centre, some area worshippers giving directly to the parish church.

Over the past two years this Area Service has experienced fifty per cent growth, from 90 to 140 weekly. Clearly the more acceptable venue of school rather than pub has contributed to this. In addition we have spelled out our 'way in' to the fellowship, by creating structures for newcomers. Ken, a builder by trade, and Derek, who is a medic, provide two useful examples of this way in. Both families made contact originally with the local church enquiring about baptism for their babies. This has proved an especially fruitful evangelistic contact in those parts of the town inhabited by young couples. Initially, enquiring parents are visited by the full-time staff member responsible for that area. The enquiry is welcomed and the Anglican alternatives of Thanksgiving or Baptism are spelled out. We offer Thanksgiving services for the birth of a child, without previous commitment by parents and at any place, day or time to suit the family. Having bent over backwards to please parents with that option, we trust they will quite understand that should they opt for Baptism – well, we expect some commitments from them.

The next step is an invitation to the Area Family Service, where the Baptism will eventually take place. Attendance at services is requested for such couples. We have also a team of Baptism visitors who will go to the home of the new family. Their task is to speak of the meaning of Baptism and of personal Christian faith. People contacted in this way, after attending Family Services for a while, are then invited along to a 'Getting-to-know-you' evening. The idea behind this is to convey the truth that Christianity is more than Sunday worship, as well as the more obvious goal of providing structures for the development of friendship. It has become clear to us that quite apart from spiritual considerations, those who stay and grow are those who find friends within the fellowship. We aim to provide structures in which such friendship can develop. We tell people in our preaching of God's love; we have then to express that love ourselves in practical ways which are socially and culturally acceptable.

The 'Getting-to-know-you' evening takes the form of a casual buffet supper. Most of those present are recent attenders at the Family Service, and two couples are the Christian hosts for the evening. The evening closes with a brief word from the Christian hosts. They explain briefly the concept of the Area Services, the vision of the parish church, the available avenues for practical ministry within the community and finally an invitation to form a Basic Christianity group for those who want to know more.

Ken and Janet, and Derek and Lynn along with others, accepted the invitation to explore the Christian faith in Basic Christianity groups. The groups that they attended were led by two different couples from within the congregation, couples who themselves have previously participated in Basic Christianity courses. Ken was the first to give his life to Christ. Week Three of the course presents the Cross, and makes the first challenge to personal repentance and faith. Janet waited until the conclusion of the course, by which time Ken was already an enthusiastic and fast-growing disciple. Derek and Lynn wanted more time to think through the implications of their course. It was some time later that their steadily growing awareness brought them to a point of clarity in their faith and the public willingness to live for Jesus.

From the Basic Christianity course, the two couples clearly needed to continue on into some longer-term group. Until then, there had been one Area-based home fellowship group for the Garden Farm people. Now, even here, growth through multiplication was needed. Human nature being what it is, there was still reluctance on the part of some members to acknowledge the need to grow. Diversifying was still seen as a threat by some. As with the Family Services earlier, so now at this smaller level the strawberry plant was putting out runners. The housegroup was divided geographically and a new job-description issued. These groups were to acknowledge a commitment among members to one another and to be open to other worshippers living within their area. They had a clear goal too, to grow to the point of multiplication again at the end of two years.

That goal has since been achieved. Derek is now joint leader of one of the home-based fellowship groups. Ken is sharing leadership of the latest Basic Christianity course. At the time of writing both of them have preached their first public sermons within the last few weeks. In connection with this they have participated in a short-term Sunday lunch-time preachers' support group, with the aim of analysing and commenting on the morning's ministry.

Growth in depth

Looking more broadly at the total ministry of the parish, growth in pastoral ministry has occurred on several fronts. Acting on the premise 'find a need and fill it' some groups have come and gone. There existed for a while a support group by the name of Passover which sought to offer some care to those returning home after a stay in hospital. A number of the Area Services, under the auspices of their Pilot Groups, run a visiting team. This team undertakes to visit, with varying degrees of regularity, elderly, bereaved and shut-in folk, not necessarily those with previous church links.

The most pioneering work in this field is that of the Night and Day Care group. This consists now of men and women who are willing to sit with the terminally ill in their homes, at all hours, providing some relief for hard-pressed relatives. The vision for this work came from the wife of one of the churchwardens, originally pursuing the possibility of hospice care for the dying. The team members are in good standing with the local medical profession who now regularly refer individuals to their care. The Night and Day team make it clear that they offer no medical experience and come in, not as substitute nursing staff, but as substitute relatives. The value of this work as an expression of the caring love of God is immense. It is true to say that the existence of this group adds a cutting edge to evangelism, exhibiting as it does something of God's concern for people and the practical effects of seeking to live for Jesus in the world.

The wider church

Links with the wider Church are also maintained. Chester-le-Street parish provides training opportunities in pastoral ministry for students from Cranmer Hall, Durham. Ian Bunting invests some of his time serving on groups influencing ministry nationally. The parish also made a step of faith and commitment to the churches of the north-east when I was seconded in the summer of 1982 to work half-time for Mission England, running training courses in Church Growth and Home Group leadership.

Where next?

What of the future? Chester-le-Street parish church has lived over the past years with dire warnings about its ability to remain unified. Each new development and experiment in strawberry-plant growth has been greeted with forebodings of disaster. Thus far the grace of God has triumphed and unity in diversity has been maintained. Under Ian Bunting's ministry uniformity of worship within the Areas has ceased and each has been allowed to blossom in a way appropriate to itself. Again, thus far, under God this has happened without a loss of the sense of belonging to one family.

With the latest addition of a monthly evening service in the community hut at Chester Moor on the very edge of the parish, the stretching of staff ministry resources is obvious. From autumn 1984 the ministry plan is to have three full-time staff members with pastoral and evangelistic responsibility for two congregations each. In addition to this there is a part-time Administrator, a part-time Parish Secretary, both recently appointed, and the Rector overseeing the whole team and its work. Area home groups are having to learn a greater degree of pastoral responsibility and care. The leaders of those groups are being affirmed in their work and equipped for their task with bi-monthly meetings together with all the staff. Preaching ministry and worship leading is increasingly being sought out and encouraged and training courses for such people will be featuring more regularly.

Perhaps the church will fulfil the prayer of some and give greater emphasis to its missionary links in three countries. We hope that its hospitality to overseas pastors studying nearby in Durham will continue. Certainly it will face the major challenge of new plant needed in the shape of a new hall for parish office accommodation and meeting rooms. Inevitably that brings with it a financial challenge of mind-boggling proportions. Prayerfully, the work of growth among individuals entering the kingdom through the door of Jesus Christ will continue to the glory of God.

Chapter 8

Bamford Chapel, Rochdale

Jeff Yates

Bamford Chapel (United Reformed Church) is situated in a rural Lancashire community close to the industrial towns of Rochdale and Heywood, a village which has grown considerably because of the extensive new properties erected for young families. In 1975 the Chapel had an average congregation of about 165, which by 1984 had grown to 300. The number of communicating members has also doubled, from 1,100 to 2,150.

The minister, the Rev. Jeffrey Yates, was educated at Little Lever Secondary Modern School, near Bolton. After two years in the textile industry and a further two years National Service he trained for the ministry of the Congregational Church and was ordained in 1959. He has served as minister of Bamford Chapel since 1975.

He is married to Sheila and they have two teenage daughters. He is a keen sportsman and has played in most of the major cricket leagues in Lancashire over the past twenty years. He also enjoys music, drama and gardening. He is deeply concerned about Church Growth and is eager to develop mission enterprise.

'To tell you the truth, I honestly thought that the only thing that could ever bring so many people together in one place was alcohol.' This was the honest assessment of a man who came to our church for the first time and was surprised to find the car park and the chapel itself full. His view of the church in general was one of a sparse gathering of fairly elderly folk, offering worship which hadn't all that much relevance to life as he knew it.

That is a similar story to many I have listened to these past nine years since settling as minister of Bamford Chapel. The building was erected in 1801 in a somewhat rural setting, in a village tucked in between the Lancashire towns of Rochdale and Heywood. It is a community not even on the map and, according to the way some statisticians judge things, not likely to be a place in which the church will grow, but where it will struggle to ward off decline.

A growing community

The village of Bamford has a population that has grown considerably in the past fifteen years or more and now numbers around six thousand. Apart from our own United Reformed Church, there is the parish church and within a mile, a large Roman Catholic church, a couple of Methodist churches and a Baptist church. The area has developed because of its accessibility to the M62 which links with the cities of Manchester and Leeds and a number of sizeable towns not too far away. Numerous young professional people now commute to their jobs, but are seeking a full involvement in their community and church. Their coming to the area has changed the nature of the neighbourhood and presented a new challenge to the Christian community.

One of the real needs of the neighbourhood since the development began has been for the sense of community. Pubs and schools apart, there are few other communal meeting places, and this presented a great opportunity to us to use the many facilities of the Chapel and its spacious grounds. By listening to God and to the people around us, we have developed some twenty-two mid-week activities designed to meet the needs of neighbours and present us with the chance of sharing the faith with them. Our premises needed modernising to meet the need and over £55,000 was raised to extend them. A large car park has also been opened.

Much work on the buildings was needed as growth began, and this in itself has called for imaginative thinking and increased giving. The nineteenth-century premises have a charm about them, but naturally require continual work to keep them in good repair. Over the past fifteen years a great deal of alteration and renovation has taken place to make the buildings suitable for worship and the mid-week organisations.

Down the years the church has been served by a long succession of most able ministers, each of whom seemed to bring his own individual style of leadership. In reading back through the minutes, magazines and brief histories of the church, one is conscious of fine service given by so many people. From conversations with older members, it is clear that they value their past life in the fellowship and they speak approvingly of their former leaders. They also reflect on difficult times and how it seemed at certain periods that things were beginning to go down. It was money from investments that kept the church solvent for quite some time, and it is only in more recent years that church finances have really begun to improve. The total financial turnover at the end of 1975 was £5,200, but the year ending 1983 saw a turnover of £25,000, with an extra £8,000 having been given for a new electronic organ in the same year. The church now gives away to world mission and other Christian work more than it raised for all purposes in 1974.

On my arrival in 1975, the average attendance of adults was around eighty, with a similar number of children. A steady growth started to take place after a year or so, and we now average over two hundred adults and some one hundred and thirty children. On certain Sundays (not always so-called 'special' ones), the numbers can soar quite considerably up towards the four hundred mark. Evening services are much smaller, with fifty to sixty in the average congregation. On those occasions when we endeavour to do something quite different, the numbers can be greatly increased. The Carol Service before Christmas in 1983 attracted over three hundred people.

Conversion growth

Since 1976, some 207 new church members have been received either by transfer or confession of faith, and well over another hundred people who are part of our family, but not yet full church members, are regular attenders. Of those received into membership, more have been received by confession of faith than by transfer. Even of those transferred to us, a number had not been attending any church for some time until they came to Bamford Chapel. With the coming of so many new people we have been greatly encouraged and challenged in the development of our life. God has answered our heartfelt prayers for his church to grow and to praise him more worthily. For this we give thanks and seek more and more to be undergirded with prayer in all that we do.

Attraction through worship

A number of changes have taken place in the field of music and drama. A small traditional choir has grown to the strength of forty and presents a wide variety of musical arrangements for worship. Under the guidance of a new and most gifted choirmaster and a talented new organist, members of the choir meet each week to prepare the music and the lead they give in weekly services has enriched the worship considerably.

Newcomers to the fellowship often comment on the high standard of musical offering. Arising out of the lead given by the choir, a Gospel Group has grown called 'Kinsfolk' who present lively music accompanied by two guitarists and, on occasions, by a violinist and pianist. The group has become well known in the area and is in demand to sing in many other places. Three cassette recordings have been made by the group and have sold well over a wide area. Congregational singing has improved greatly as a result of the praise offered by the choir and gospel singers.

After a visit from 'The Riding Lights' theatre company from York, a team of excellent actors from our own fellowship began to develop exciting and attractive drama productions. The chapel has a moveable pulpit and offers a most suitable area for drama to be presented. New stage units were bought to enable different sets to be erected for the use of imaginative drama. Excellent productions have resulted in recent years and it is hoped that this form of dramatic presentation will be further developed.

A Junior Choir has also led worship and singing from our youth organisations, and soloists have also provided variety and inspiration. There is weekly sharing in the conduct of worship by those who read lessons, lead prayers, present statements of faith, take part in interviews and on occasions give the addresses and sermons. The aim is for all present to be as involved in the worship as possible and this has been done through dance and other expressions of joyful sharing.

There is evidence to show how those who have been drawn to our fellowship have been motivated to tell others of how they have found blessing in Christ through sharing in the life of the church. I met a vicar in Rochdale who told me how one of our women had spoken to him about the value of belonging to our church. He was impressed by her sincere expression of faith. What he did not know was that the woman concerned was quite a new convert to our fold, and how gratified I was to know of her open witness. When people are prepared to talk openly about how belonging to the church is helping them to live, others will start to take notice. A good many folk have come to look at our church as a result of our members being willing to talk about their faith and how they have found new life in Jesus.

One man told us he first came out of sheer despair after his father had died. He had never been in the habit of going to church, but this morning he decided to come to one of our services. Some time later, when training to be a church member, he explained his feelings in this way: 'I came not knowing quite why, but once in the church I felt moved by the friendliness of the worship and the meaningfulness of the message.' That man is now one of our most dedicated youth workers and his life has blossomed in quite special ways.

Quite often people join us who are wanting to give religion another try after long periods of feeling disappointed by what was offered to them in their earlier years. When they have their children or want a new sense of purpose, they try the church again, and, if it satisfies their longing, will commit themselves to Jesus. It has been most illuminating to sit and listen to so many who have expressed how coming out of a spiritual wilderness back into the life of the church has given them a fresh zest for living.

Meeting felt needs

It has been our aim to see a need and to fill it. As people have

joined us, we have asked them what they wanted us to offer
to meet their need, rather than impose on them
organisations that simply suited us. By our willingness to do
this, we have recruited quite a lot of people and engaged
them in providing the drive and leadership to get new groups
off the ground. In more ways than one, it has been revealing
to observe how quite new members of our fellowship have
been prepared to do things after only a short time with us. It
could be that sometimes growth is not seen in some areas
because we forbid people to exercise any leadership until
they have been with us for a prescribed period. It is worth
remembering that some young professional people may only
stay in an area for a limited time, and if every church they
join refuses to use their gifts, they may well give up in
frustration!

Every service and activity is seen as an opportunity to
reach people with the love of Jesus. The many infant
baptisms and weddings held in the church are carefully
prepared for and followed up. The work of the Cradle Roll
secretary is undertaken with loving zeal so that young
parents are made to feel they and their new child matter.
Expressions of caring through the worship and visits enhance
the work. Each year a special Cradle Roll Service is held,
followed by afternoon tea and a time to meet church officials.
The Mums and Babies group grew out of this work and for a
number of our events it is now quite natural for us to provide
crèche facilities so that our young families can be together.

With an average of thirty weddings a year – an increasing
figure – there is ample opportunity provided for counselling
couples and offering the friendship of the church to all who
attend the services of marriage. A lot of care and attention is
given to all who come to such services and some have joined
us as a consequence.

Outreach is also seen in terms of conducting a short
service once a fortnight in a local home for the elderly. This
service means much to the residents and our people are most
welcome in the home. Other groups in the church visit other
homes and societies in the area to extend Christian
fellowship, all of which has its spin-off for good.

Wide horizons

A determined effort has been made to widen horizons amongst our members as far as mission and the world Church is concerned. Over recent years we have had a policy of bringing denominational leaders and missionaries to our fellowship to share their vision and experience with us, and for them to have a glimpse of what God is doing among the dark Satanic mills of Lancashire! These exchanges have been beneficial and we do have a clearer picture of the Church in all the world and feel inspired to offer more support in prayer and money. One of our young people was sponsored by the church to visit Zambia and others are encouraged to attend missionary conferences and other learning situations. Links have been forged with a Presbyterian Church in Ohio as a result of the minister and his family spending a period there. Since their visit the links have been strengthened by further visits of elders and members. Out of all this has come a willingness to learn more about the world mission of the Church.

Regular prayer is offered and increased efforts made to raise money for the spreading of the glorious gospel. There is constant emphasis on the preaching and teaching ministry of the church towards mission, and this has begun to bear fruit.

Mid-week activities

The numerous mid-week activities attract quite different people. We offer sporting recreation to our young community, simply because there is a need for it: tennis, badminton, pool, table tennis, football, cricket, indoor bowls and keep-fit are all available. Our aim is to present a balanced faith and to help people be fit in body, mind and spirit. There are those who start off on our tennis courts but by God's grace and personal witnessing, end up in the courts of the Lord.

The youth programme is designed to reach children and young people through uniformed organisations (Boys' and Girls' Brigade, Brownies and Guides) and also through open youth clubs known as 913 Club and Youth Fellowship. Two Sunday night groups, Koinonia and Hay-Hodos offer a

spiritual programme that runs alongside the educational
teaching of Junior Church. Some two hundred young people
participate in our weekly activities which are led by keen and
talented leaders who are all committed members of the
church and who are ever evaluating their .vork and seeking
to be trained for it. A Youth Leaders' Council helps the work
to be co-ordinated and is now supported by a group of elders,
whose responsibility it is to monitor the work and encourage
and help those involved.

Welcoming newcomers

Newcomers' evenings have been an important feature in
attracting new members and helping them settle in. At
monthly intervals groups of eight to ten newcomers are
invited to the Manse for an evening to meet the minister and
his wife and at least one elder and his or her spouse. These
informal meetings prove beneficial in assessing how best the
church can help people and in gauging what kind of talents
they are likely to be able to offer in the life of the church.
Over the years a tremendous amount of good has come out
of these get-togethers to offer friendship and outline what the
church can offer. Such evenings have been followed up by
meals provided by the whole church to welcome newcomers
and to introduce them to church officers. A remark
frequently made by folk new to the fellowship is, 'I was made
to feel so welcome when I came.' The reputation of being a
friendly welcoming church can be a real asset in continuing
to grow.

People new to the church are visited as soon as possible by
the minister, who may then arrange for other elders and
members to call as well. An increasing number of members
are happy to share in this ministry of visitation and that
presents the community with the feeling that others do care
for them. Out of the Luncheon Club work, much visiting is
done by the dedicated team who organise the Club so
lovingly. Lonely and housebound people in the community
who are referred to us are brought for lunch each week and
those who join us in this way are followed up in a most caring
manner by those who give leadership to the Club.

The development of this work has been very important in

our understanding of the needs of older people. In a church
where less than a sixth of the members are over pensionable
age, we feel it essential to care for those who are growing
older. As the leader of the Club says,

> 'We have a good mix of members. Some are very old and
> frail, in their late eighties and early nineties; others are
> active, in their seventies and early eighties. We find the
> mix is valuable as the vigorous members bring news and
> liveliness to those with more restricted lives and also help
> them move about from room to room. The value to the
> members is that the housebound are given transport and a
> chance to move out of their own homes and the
> newcomers to the district meet new friends and integrate
> into the community more readily. The helpers have also
> gained from their involvement with the Club.'

Active involvement

The involvement mentioned by the leader of the Luncheon
Club is one of the key factors of our general growth. It is
always our policy to get people involved in doing something
for the Lord as quickly as possible. We do not encourage
'spectatoritis' which causes people just to sit and watch
others doing things. As quickly as possible, having assessed
the gifts people have, we encourage them to serve the Lord.
So often in our churches, we tend to keep people waiting in
the wings too long before allowing them on stage. This is not
our policy, even though at times we have encountered
certain difficulties where newcomers have not always fulfilled
what we thought was their leadership potential. Overall,
though, we would claim a measure of success in assessing
potential leaders and helping their development. We now
have an excellent team of trained and dedicated leaders in all
aspects of our work. There is a desire for shared leadership
and this we encourage. When people have that level of
commitment and intend putting their faith into service, this
means they have truly settled in the church.

It may well be that because we use so many committed
leaders in the weekly programme of the church, we have not
been able to set up the numerous house groups others claim

to have. Rather than have people meeting for study and discussion, we favour the method of involving them in actual training to do something in terms of helping others. By being involved in teaching, drama, music, visitation, leading young people's groups and the like, a large proportion of those who might gravitate towards a housegroup are too busy to do so. Therefore while we have three continuing housegroups, one for weekly Bible study, one for general themes of study and discussion and the other a Prayer Circle, we would not point to housegroups as such figuring significantly in our growth. When a church has the sort of mid-week programme of activities we provide, it is evidence from our experience that housegroups are not needed. Most of our members are already involved in mid-week events either as leaders or participants and therefore enjoy fellowship on a weekly basis with others, as well as in worship on a Sunday.

Membership preparation

The receiving in of over two hundred members has afforded the opportunity for regular classes to train those wishing to join the church. No one has been received in without attending a series of classes with the minister to consider what belonging to the church entails. These times of training have been most important and, on occasions, groups who have come together have gained much from their own open sharing of faith and experience. The demands of following Jesus and being engaged in the mission of the church have caused many to think deeply about their overall commitment and prompted action to support the decision they have made.

Perhaps the thing we have to grapple with most in the future development of the church is that of nurturing those who have joined us. To our sadness, we have had our losses and disappointments. Some joined us with enthusiasm but their promise has fizzled out. Others who we thought could have played a significant part in the life of the fellowship have had no staying power or capacity to relate to a large number of other talented people. Personality clashes have taken place and sometimes a lack of maturity has led to painful departures. Some who were big fish in a small pond were not able to cope with being a not-so-big fish in a larger one. For those who assume that growth is all sweetness and light, the facts need spelling out, that times of tension and misunderstanding can also be experienced in a growing church. When many new people arrive, all sorts of hares can be set running and much prayerful and patient loving is necessary to enable people to join in true fellowship. Loving and mature leadership is required to bring the best out of those whom God in his infinite wisdom has brought together to be his Body.

Visitation

Regular visiting is a feature of the church's day-to-day life. As one who sees wisdom in the old saying 'A homegoing parson makes for a churchgoing people', I believe in the importance of regular visiting. Over the years I have tried to fit in a great many visits each week to the sick, elderly, housebound, bereaved and new residents. This has paid dividends as people have expressed appreciation of the visits and been willing to talk about themselves and how they feel about the church. Because the minister visits, others are encouraged to do so, and the community experiences the sense of a caring church. Those who do the visiting learn much and the entire work of the church is blessed.

An attractive leaflet giving details of our worship and weekly programme is circulated from time to time and then followed up by a visit. At Christmas and at other times of the year we distribute information about what we plan to do and invite our neighbours to join us. Personal invitation is also something we constantly stress to our members, so that they will encourage new neighbours and friends to come. Quite a number in fact have joined us in this way, as they have responded to a friendly invitation from our members. It has been most encouraging to see how those who have found help in living for Christ, have been keen to tell others of what they have found.

Further outreach

Our outreach has included providing outings for such groups as the local Stroke Club and Mentally Handicapped Society, culminating in an act of worship. Local schools have been invited to share in worship with their choirs. Special events have been staged with the whole community in mind and this has helped us reach a wider number of people. The appeal of our musical and dramatic methods of presenting the gospel has attracted others to us. No opportunity is missed, if we can help it, of making our neighbours aware of our existence and of the sense of joy and meaningful life we experience as followers of Jesus.

Family parties and sports evenings and days have helped to create a sense of being a family in Christ. Entertaining other church fellowships, and welcoming visitors to our homes, has widened our horizons. District events are often held at Bamford because of the extensive grounds and facilities we are able to provide and this makes for wider contacts. It has been our endeavour to be open and welcoming to all who wish to come to us and this has resulted in our entertaining a great variety of God's people.

Releasing resources to the wider church

Changes in leadership occur in a fellowship that grows. Almost every church office has changed hands in recent years. When vacancies for jobs arise, they are quickly filled by eager folk willing to do them. This means that we can encourage people to be released to serve in other ways if we consider their gifts can be better used. It has also meant that we have been able to release people to serve our two neighbouring U.R.C. churches in Heywood and Norden and consequently to develop closer links with them. Members and elders have also been released to do important work at district and national level and this has proved beneficial to them and to the wider life of the church.

The request from other churches to share something of our developing life with them, has led to some strange experience. As one who has accepted many such requests to talk about aspects of growth, I have found quite different reactions. Perhaps it is that we have grown so accustomed to decline that we simply do not know how to handle growth at any level? On occasions one meets people who seem to be resentful that a measure of growth is taking place. Others accuse you of fabricating the facts or of over-glamourising your situation, or even suggest that things are so favourable in your area that you just could not fail to show some signs of growth! When you point out that theirs and many other situations are similar to your own but little seems to have happened, uneasy tensions may arise. Indeed, there have been times when having got home from such meetings I have vowed never again to accept any further engagements to talk about what I have seen God doing. But I know how wrong such an attitude is, for if here and there one can share a vision and stimulate others to try something new, time has been well spent.

I recall how much I was helped myself by attending a Church Growth conference led by Eddie Gibbs and Roy Pointer. Their enthusiasm in presenting the challenge, and their expertise in showing how growth might take place, were so enlightening and helpful. It is important that where we can, we should share with others the things God has been doing in our local churches, in the hope that others might capture a vision and do great work for the Lord.

There may well be a slightly painful side to growth which needs to be understood. If we become so obsessed with decline that any kind of growth makes us suspicious, we need the help of others to lift us on to a different plane. In the first instance, this may be a somewhat painful experience as it calls us to look at new opportunities and perhaps to give up doing some things we had always felt were important. This can be disturbing to us, but it may also be the way that leads to new life and growth. If God is to do a new thing in the life of the church we belong to, he will need to change us and point us in the ways he wants us to travel.

One church springing to new life in a community and giving the glory to God (for all the glory must be his) can in time influence other local and district churches for good. I don't believe any church can ever grow to itself alone. The very fact of its growth will challenge others to consider new ways of serving God. Over the past four years, three of our members have offered themselves for the work of the Christian ministry. It is over forty years since anyone from the fellowship did that. Our students, who leave us for college and university, have been playing a not insignificant part in the religious life to which they have moved. Our Gospel Group has brought a breath of fresh air to many a church. Our choir has been instrumental in making others see again the power of Christian music in the life of the church. Through drama and excellent lay preaching and all sorts of other expressions of outreach, people near and far have found bessing. Some of those won for Christ while with us are now doing mighty things in other areas to which they have moved. In these and other ways, God has forced us out to witness in many places and we praise him for everything he has done. We now even have links with Christians in the United States through exchanges and we have hosted visits for Christians from many parts of the world. For a community once not on any map, something of our life is now known afar, and God be praised for what he has moved us to do.

Leadership demands

There has been some little adjustment to be made along the way. For a pastor who places emphasis upon a personal caring ministry, I have had to realise that one cannot care on the same level for three or four hundred in the way one used to care for one hundred. Style of leadership has had to be wrestled with, the sharing of responsibilities has had to be worked out – and is still being worked out. Not to know everybody personally comes hard, but can be a challenge also to develop more effective leadership. Learning to delegate is essential. Learning to trust the devoted leadership of others is good for the soul. Seeing things happen because others have taken the initiative is liberating, even if mistakes are sometimes made because of over-enthusiasm or lack of experience. In a church which is coming alive and attracting many different types of personalities, waters will on occasions be ruffled and disturbances occur, but these are problems of life not death, and they are exciting problems to be dealing with. When the Spirit gives life, what may have

been tranquil for a time will be different, but it will also be
exciting, as people discover the many ways God works
through his children.

Of course we have made mistakes, and some of them we
regret. Amidst all the busyness and the thrill of seeing so
many new people, there have been moments of loneliness,
feelings of sheer inadequacy, periods of bewilderment as one
thing after another has been set in motion to meet the needs
of those who have come amongst us. With a Manse adjoined
to a church which is busy seven days a week, I can easily
become quite drained and envy those who knew the chapel in
the days of its rural tranquillity. In any growing situation
one experiences attacks on one's leadership, suffering the
sniping of those who resent change, even envy from some
people, because such things never happened when they were
in positions of leadership. Human nature is a strange thing
and can show peculiar sides in certain situations. But all that
said, God has sustained us through the period of growth and
given us cause for rejoicing. There are those who have come
through it feeling all the better for it. Certainly they are more
flexible, more humble, more aware of how mighty things can
happen when they, and others, respond to the leading of the
Spirit and are committed to the Lord.

Looking to the future

We now experience a sense of shared leadership. A forward-
looking community is more ready and capable of planning
ahead. Financial burdens have been lifted but we need much
extra income to cope with what is envisaged for the future.
There is much more to be done on the teaching side of the
church, and we pray for guidance to develop more
satisfactorily the pastoral and educational side of our life. A
deepening of the prayer life of the church, and of Bible study
and biblical exposition, are areas we have much more to
learn about.

But we are open to learn. We are ready for any new thrust
the Lord calls us to make. Later this year we intend, with our
Anglican friends, to do an extensive house-to-house
visitation to tie in with Mission England. It is our heartfelt
desire to 'hear what the Lord is saying to the churches' and

to respond to all he is saying to our local church as well.

We recognise that in spite of all that has happened and is continuing to happen, we are as yet only scratching the surface of things, but we are equally encouraged that it is not 'alcohol' that regularly brings three to four hundred people together to worship and to share in a programme of study, fellowship, enjoyment and exercise; it is the vitality of God's Spirit working in us all. We have witnessed God's power working among us and we look to the future in cheerful expectancy, believing that he has yet mighty things to do through us.

Chapter 9

St Helens Elim Pentecostal Church

David Tinnion

The Elim Pentecostal Church is situated in the town centre of St Helens, Merseyside, at the heart of a declining industrial area with a large unemployment problem. Its congregation however is on the increase: from 125 total attendance on an average Sunday in 1975 to 540 in 1984.

The Rev. David Tinnion was born in Carlisle in 1946. After leaving school he worked for West Cumberland Farmers in administration, and trained for the ministry at the Elim Bible College, Capel, Surrey from 1969–71.

Much of his time apart from the ministry at St Helens is taken up with convention speaking and ministers' seminars, but when time allows he enjoys walking in the Lake District and Snowdonia.

St Helens is traditionally the centre of the world's glass industry, but it is now an industrial town with high unemployment. Bordering the City of Liverpool, it is a Metropolitan Borough with a population of 190,000 (1981) nearly seventy per cent of whom belong to the Roman Catholic Church.

From small beginnings

The Elim Pentecostal Church in St Helens was established many years ago and originally met in various hired halls. One was Milton Chambers, in the town centre. The building was shared with the Jehovah's Witnesses and the Church of the Latter-Day Saints (Mormons) who were also pioneering in the town.

During the 1950s, T. E. Francis was minister of the Elim Church in Wigan and, through his help, a plot of land was purchased in Duke Street, then a heavily-populated part of the town near the centre. A small hall, kitchen and toilets were erected. This first building was to be the Minor Hall; the main church was to be erected when money was available. The cost of the project was £1,300. At that time, building material was in short supply and Pastor Francis, in his little old van, went around collecting such things as window frames and doors, which were virtually unobtainable at that time. The work was hard and the small congregation had many set-backs and disappointments. Sometimes attendance was as low as three persons.

In 1966, Pastor and Mrs Jack Tetchner, who had recently retired, were asked to look after the small congregation. They travelled three times a week from Southport to St Helens to minister to the church. On their first Sunday morning there were four people in the congregation and that evening, ten. In both services there was just one man, who today is still the Organist and Treasurer.

The work began to grow and the vision that Pastor Francis had for the main church came into being during the ministry of Jack Tetchner. It was a real step of faith for the small congregation, but they were people of faith and vision directed by God-given leadership. The church was built for a total of £10,000 and was opened by Lord Pilkington on 10 March 1973.

On Saturday, November 2 1974, I was inducted at St Helens. It was a happy occasion, with part of the congregation coming from my previous pastorate in Driffield, Humberside. Pastor Tetchner felt that it was then time for retiring (for the second time!) at the age of seventy-two, and was pleased to have seen the new church built and the congregation grow; he felt that it was right to hand over to a younger man.

I had not moved church before and was full of mixed emotions. I knew that I was in God's will, but the environment was so different from that from which I had just

come, and from the beauty of the Lake District where I was
born and brought up. The church was surrounded by acres
of dereliction. Over three thousand terraced houses in the
district were ear-marked for demolition, so that the whole
area was in a state of decay. Today, ten years later, the
church is surrounded by a wilderness of waste ground
waiting to be developed. We have purchased a large site on
one of the cleared areas to build a new church centre.

On my first Sunday, the church had many empty seats.
The people were lovely and kind, but I longed to see every
place filled. One morning I felt compelled to pray over every
seat in the church. I prayed that in the months and years to
come many people would find Christ as Saviour. That
prayer is still being answered.

During the last ten years 370 people have been baptised as
believers. The church has a regular congregation of nearly
200 people at the Sunday morning and evening services. The
All-age Christian Education Programme before the morning
service has an average attendance of 180 adults and children.

Sacrificial giving

The average weekly offering ten years ago was £35; now it is
nearly £800, including covenants. Gifts to the Building
Fund, along with giving to missions, are separate from this
amount. An appeal for finance is only mentioned once a year
at the Annual General Meeting, held every January, when
new projects and plans are announced by the elders.

The church is situated in an area of very high
unemployment, with only one-third of the congregation
classified as wage earners. A number of years ago, the
church had to lease some of its land to help pay some of the
running costs. Now, we pay two full-time Pastors and are
about to commence a building project which is going to cost
just over £300,000.

The growth over the last ten years has been gradual. The
size of the building has deterred the fellowship from having
special events or inviting 'big names'. The growth has come
from the members' inviting friends and contacts to the
church's activities. Fifty per cent of the fellowship have come
to know Christ through people inviting them to the church.

Although we have had an overcrowding problem for a number of years, it has not deterred the leadership from developing new programmes of ministry. The church hires two floors of the nearby Y.M.C.A. building every Sunday morning, for some of its All-age Christian Education departments. A great emphasis is placed on commitment to the local body and this is seen in the giving, tremendous for a high-unemployment blackspot. I would agree with Michael Green: 'True giving is an overflow. It does not have to be extracted painfully from our unwilling pocket books. It flows out of hearts that have been warmed by the Lord's love.'

Significant areas of change

In the last few years, there have been three areas of tremendous change: the introduction of All-age Christian Education, the commencement of a housegroup ministry, and the worship.

1. *All-age Christian Education*. Seven years ago, the church changed from a traditional, afternoon Sunday School to an All-age total-hour programme using Scripture Press material. The changeover was made gradually, with the Sunday School being departmentalised before moving to Sunday morning. The church premises are far from adequate, but the kitchen was turned into a 'Cradle Roll' area for babies, with a nursing staff in charge; the garage at the rear of the church was made into a temporary hall for the Juniors.

Over the years the education work has developed, with departments for all ages from babies right through to a class for adults who study the Bible all the way through every nine years. The teachers are trained and attend various teacher-training conferences. The programme is administered by four Superintendents and two Transport Officers. The Superintendents meet four times a year with me, and monthly with their own department teachers. The whole teaching staff hold two joint meetings a year for major direction and prayer.

The staff of nearly thirty people are looking forward to the new building, where an eight-department programme can be held under one roof. When the new centre opens, it will seat 500 people and it will be able to accommodate an Education Programme for 350 apart from the main worship area. The large car park will accommodate at least fifty cars, and adjoining car parks will bring the total space to around two hundred vehicles.

The church has, besides the All-age programme, a strong Youth Group which come together on each Tuesday evening for their own spiritual meeting, under the leadership of a young man I led to Christ in my previous church.

Mid-week activities for children have never been very successful because of the lack of houses surrounding the church, and most of the concentration among youth and children has been given to the All-age programme and the senior youth work. Now that houses are beginning to be built and a new community is emerging the church is at present training leaders to run Campaigner Clans for children and teenagers.

2.*Housegroups.* Five years ago, the church began to form housegroups. Meetings were held monthly at first but, after two years, it was felt that there was no sense of continuity and that, if the cell groups were to fulfil their ministry of teaching, follow-up and outreach in different locations of the town, they would have to be more frequent. The housegroups have now found a 'level' with meetings held every week – except one each month when a Celebration is held in the church itself. The Church Prayer Meeting is held every Saturday morning, at seven-thirty a.m., and various other prayer meetings are held on other evenings and also during the day.

The leaders of the housegroups are given training and are asked to write a weekly report for the eldership. The housegroups are now a vital part of the church's ministry. Follow-up and outreach are arranged through the groups. Sometimes, two or more groups will get together for a specific project or social event. The eldership meets with the group leaders on a regular basis, for encouragement and direction, but the group leaders have full responsibility for the groups and arrange the programmes. A group is divided when it gets too large, and when a leader has been trained to shepherd the new group; direction is given by the eldership at the monthly Celebration. The weekly meeting in the locality is just part of a group's activity: the group in a particular area functions seven days a week by caring, teaching, follow-up and evangelism.

The desire of the leadership is to see that people are brought into Christian maturity, 'So that we may present everyone perfect in Christ' (Col. 1:28). I am convinced that a properly-run housegroup is one of the best ways to bring people into maturity, to evangelise the local area and bring people through into leadership.

In the small group, people can develop ministries and gifts. They are encouraged to partake in prayer and praise, to be free in worship, to exercise spiritual gifts and to give short sermons. Just having a housegroup is not enough; it must be linked to the church, its membership and leadership. The cell is not a unit on its own; it is linked to the body. We have found that to run properly-organised housegroups we have had to invest time, patience and teaching to see the programme grow. The minister of the world's largest church, in South Korea, Dr. Paul Yonggi Cho, says, 'Just organising a programme in your church will not ensure its continued success. You must take a continual and active role in its implementation and motivation.'

The housegroup is the place where potential leaders can gain experience. Ministries emerge and are encouraged to develop. The group leaders are exercising a parenthood ministry and should have a mother-and-father spirit: 'Like a mother caring for her little children' (I Thess. 2:7) and 'As a father deals with his own children' (I Thess. 2:11). It has been found that it costs to bring up a family. 'Guard what has been entrusted to your care.' (I Tim. 6:20).

3. *Worship.* Musically the worship has changed gradually over the last ten years from an organ and piano to a worship band of brass, percussion, string and woodwind. They lead the worship, which is very free, with the spiritual songs appearing on an overhead projector screen. In most services the hymn book is also used. We have learned that there is a difference between singing choruses, even though they are from scripture, and true heart-felt worship. When we gather

for our worship we have learned to 'enter into his gates with thanksgiving and into his courts with praise' (Ps. 100:4).

We gather together for a purpose. When the church met at Antioch, something happened. We see in Acts 13:2 that there was a prophecy. Some churches meet and nothing happens. C. H. Spurgeon said, 'I would sooner risk the danger of a tornado of religious excitement than see the air grow stagnant with dead formality.'

In most services, the gifts of the Spirit are exercised: people are given an opportunity to take part in the services, although the services are directed by the eldership. The worship is very spontaneous – sometimes loud and very exuberant, sometimes quiet and passive.

Continuous Evangelism

A number of years ago I realised in my planning that, if I expected God to answer my prayers for growth and believed that many people would come to know Christ, I must plan so that the 'fruit would remain'. I knew that I must devise a simple plan that would help to preserve the fruit. I called it the 'Three C's' – Contact, Commitment and Continuation.

The church has a continuous programme of evangelism, through the housegroups, the Sunday services and through the Friday evening evangelism team, which visits the public houses, clubs and parks in the town. Contacts are being made all the time, with the purpose of inviting those without Christ to the Sunday gathering. When a person attends the church for the first time, he or she is handed a 'Welcome Packet' at a convenient part of the service. In the packet there are various kinds of literature: gospel tracts, the church magazine and a letter from the ministry team explaining the type of service. If a person responds to a gospel appeal, and is counselled after the service, he or she is given some suitable follow-up material in an envelope. In these two – the Welcome and New Christian Packets – there are reply slips to fill in and these are given, after completion, to the ministry team. This method is used at various outreaches the church sponsors from time to time. The address is given to the local housegroup leader, who makes sure that the person receives an invitation to the next housegroup meeting and is consistently followed up by the group.

The church holds continuous classes for those who desire to know about it and its ministry. Having come to the church and become Christians, they are invited to attend a commitment course called 'A Firm Foundation'.

Building relationships

The church is seen not as a place for people to come to for a 'shot in the arm', or to get 'charged up' like a car battery, but as a body of related people who have been joined together to become a 'spiritual body' moving forward in the same direction. People must be committed to a local body. The eight-week 'Firm Foundation' course is a basic teaching course for those desiring to know what it means to belong to the fellowship. (After the course, the participants have the opportunity to apply for church membership, and their application is considered by the eldership.) The basic foundations of the Christian life are explained and those on the course are free to ask questions and join in discussion. Various subjects are covered on the course, including Salvation, Water Baptism, Baptism in the Holy Spirit, Faith, Prayer, Bible-reading, Satan, Worship, Relationships, Church Life and Structure, Tithing and the Second Coming. The course is linked to the local housegroups and the people receive as much help as possible to enable them to develop their Christian lives.

New people are received into membership on a Sunday morning at the Communion service. It is always a happy occasion. In the afternoon, the new members and leaders have tea together. If a person has been a member of another church, a letter is sent informing the minister of that church that the person has requested membership of the Elim Church. Every effort is made to see that a right relationship is kept with other churches. We have been accused of sheep-stealing on many occasions, but we make every effort to keep the unity of the Spirit. Over sixty people have left other local churches of various denominations to join the Elim Church, mainly because they were attracted by the expository preaching and the vibrant worship.

Growing people

Jack W. Hayward of the 'Church on the Way' in Van Nuys,
California, says that he is more interested in growing 'big
people' than in building a big church. Our desire must be to
have people who are going to have an effect on the local
community. We may not be content to have a mission every
so often, but must be a mission all the time. How dare we
blame the world if it is the fault of the church? We must let
our light shine and scatter the salt in our local community.
So often, churches are content to hold services instead of to
be Christ's witnesses.

Priorities

As I look towards the future I see four priorities:

1. *The church must have a purpose in what it is doing.* The
purpose of our fellowship is to express the life of Christ.

> God always wants to have a place, a community, which
> belongs to Him really and truly, so that God's being can
> dwell there. God needs a place from where He can work
> for the rest of the world. There must be a place on the
> Earth from where the sun of God's Kingdom shines forth.
> (Christoph Blumhardt)

It is very important that as leaders, we know in what
direction we are going. The church is in fellowship with the
World-wide Pentecostal Movement, but we are only a
movement if we keep moving: if we do not, we will end up as
a monument.

In recent years much of my time has been taken up with
the building project. It would have been easy just to have
concentrated on the fabric, furniture and the finance and to
have forgotten that we are, first of all, called to be 'fishers of
men'. As a church, our purpose is not only to be a place
where the glory of God is seen and felt, but a place of
continual evangelism in the town. 'Evangelism is the normal
life of the Church and can never be an optional extra' (Joost
de Blank).

The leaders meet weekly to pray and to plan the church's

programme and direction. We realise that we cannot lead the flock from the middle. We cannot take the people any further than we are prepared to go ourselves and that means we have to be in unity. Psalm 133 points out, 'How good and pleasant it is when brothers live together in unity . . . for there the Lord bestows his blessing.'

We meet together regularly to pray for those God has put under our care. This is a great responsibility and we need that continual infilling of the Holy Spirit that we may present 'All men mature in Christ'.

2. *The church must have people who have a right relationship with one another.* It is very important that all members are rightly related to one another. To do our work properly our fellowship must be a Body that is healthy, with every part functioning properly. Have you ever thought what ministry Christ would have had if his body had been paralysed? He would never have been able to put his arms around the sick, speak words of comfort to the sad and walk to the homes of sinners. He was only able to do these because he had a healthy body. So many churches never grow because they are paralysed by division, discord and jealousy.

When people visit the church they sense the tremendous love there is to be found among the people. That does not say that differences and problems never arise but, instead of the wounds festering, they are treated. The housegroups are a great help in keeping unity within the Body. Problems can go unnoticed for weeks in a large congregation but, in a small closely-knit group, it is hard to hide one's feelings. There are no back seats and you cannot hide behind your hymn book in a housegroup.

We can try to organise blessing around choruses, choirs, committees and conferences, but what really works is an anointed, liberated Body.

For years, many churches have left the clergy to do the work of the ministry while most Christians watch. When a person attends the commitment classes at the St Helens Elim Church, however, one of the evenings is spent on how the people can serve and function in the local Body. We endeavour to mobilise all of the membership. We hold a number of training seminars throughout the year, so that people can be encouraged to find their places in the Body.

If a person has a real gift for evangelism, he or she is encouraged to join the evangelistic team under the leadership of Co-Pastor Stephen Derbyshire, who was once a drug addict and came to know Christ six years ago one Sunday evening in the church. The team, as they visit, distribute tracts entitled 'Good News for St Helens', which include Stephen's testimony.

3. *The church must have a programme that is relevant.* We have had to be prepared to abandon structures, strategies and schemes that have outgrown their usefulness. Some people have had to step down to allow ministries to emerge. So often the Church today gives money for projects and not for personnel. We must remember that, as Samuel Chadwick said: 'The Holy Ghost does not anoint machinery but men. He does not work through organisations but through men.'

Before our new building could be erected, about thirty small houses had to be demolished. Similarly, we have had to remove some of our worn-out traditions and structures so that a right foundation could be laid. We are constantly reviewing our programme. When a programme is no longer useful it should be buried. Some things, like the Word of God, never change: change is disastrous if employed purely for its own sake. All our changes must be led by the Spirit. In fact, everything we do must have a spiritual point to it. Change is not sufficient if there is no life. You can do anything you like with a corpse, but it will do nothing of itself because it is dead.

I have learned that in order for us to grow and have a larger programme of activity, the leadership base must be extended. The concept of sharing the ministry is very threatening to some ministers. To me, it is a great joy to work alongside men with different ministries, submitted and committed to each other – men who know in what direction they are moving.

As we look to the future, we are going to build upon the programme that has been established already and implement many new programmes because of the new facilities.

We are considering a programme of establishing new churches in the area. We shall concentrate on responsive areas. Strategic positioning of personnel can play a vital part in the advancement of the gospel and the establishment of new fellowships. In our church planting, we must not sever the cutting until it has established its roots and its life can be sustained.

Gipsy Smith said, 'To send an evangelist to some deserted, disorganised chapel, situated somewhere perhaps in a godless wilderness, and then expect valuable results in a week, is like sending a man to gather apples in the Sahara Desert.'

Within the church at the present are teams who will be used in the materialising of new works. There is an evangelistic team, who will work alongside the pioneer personnel, and a musical team. We are encouraging the children to learn musical instruments at school, so that they can be used in the music ministry in the future. It is so important to work in a team. People in leadership positions get disappointed and disheartened. It is vital that, when pressures and problems do arise, we can share them with the team.

4. *The church must have property that can be a tool to serve the needs of the Body.* We thank God for the opportunity that has been given to us to build a church centre. We see the building not as a temple, but as a tool. We are building because of a need. We are making room to provide for the needs of a growing, healthy Body.

As the church began to grow, the leaders recognised the need for larger facilities. A number of properties were considered along with extending our present property. Doors kept closing but, all the time, as we continued to pray, we knew that God had a perfect plan.

The local Council offered us the choice of three large sites to build a church centre. We knew that this would be a great financial commitment, but God has proved himself to be faithful and the people have given generously.

The centre is to be open throughout the day, as well as the evening, for different activities. It is an answer to the desire to reach the new community being built around it – meeting many social needs, but primarily always being part of the commission to win people for Christ.

In the new premises, there is to be a prayer chapel where people can gather throughout the day, as well as a training centre, which will be fully equipped with the latest audio-visual aids, and a printing press to produce our own tracts and publications. A playgroup, coffee lounge and bookshop are also included in the project. Plans are also under way to have events for the unemployed, senior citizens' luncheon clubs and a telephone 'help' ministry.

It would be wrong for us to say that we have arrived. We feel we have only run the first lap. We are still not a large church, but we are aware of tremendous vision and enthusiasm; if we continue to grow at our present rate, we believe that we shall, under God, have a tremendous effect on the town.

We are just beginning to 'Take the Land'. Like Joshua, we look to the future and we say, 'There remaineth yet very much land to be possessed,' but believe that a good foundation has been laid for a harvest of souls.

There have been two important contributing factors to the growth of the church: firstly, the fact that the church has had in nearly twenty years only two Pastors, (three, including Stephen Derbyshire who became Co-Pastor this year), and secondly, the relationships the leaders have with each other.

The person in the street is not really interested in our theological positions or what is written in our constitutions, but he or she does ask, 'Does it work?' When people come into contact with the fellowship in Duke Street, they see lives that have been changed . . . all joined together in the unity of the Spirit, an anointed body of God's people.

Chapter 10

Canford Magna Parish Church

Ian Savile

The village of Canford Magna, near Wimborne, Dorset, has been substantially increased by the addition of housing estates to accommodate the population overflow from Poole, Wimborne and Bournemouth. About 25% of the housing in the village is council-owned. Accurate figures are not available for congregational attendance at the parish church (Church of England), but the congregation and the number of communicants have doubled over the period 1975–1984.

The Rev. Ian Savile, the minister, was educated at public school and was commissioned in the Royal Artillery and the Royal Indian Artillery. He trained for the ministry at Cambridge University. He is married to a former school teacher, and they have three teenage children. His principal interests are family life, military history, leadership and jigsaws.

1971 and all that

The story of a church is always one about the ongoing purposes of God, and it is difficult to break into the sequence to make a start. However, 1971 seems a good place, both because it saw a change of Vicar, and also because it coincided with the beginning of the new housing estates which now make the bulk of our population.

When the new Vicar, John Collins, arrived, he found a delightful parish church dating from Saxon and Norman times, in the middle of a parish area stretching three miles either side of the church and two and a half miles from north to south. Most of it was still farm or heath land. The church was once the only church for the whole Poole area, the area covered by the Saxon manor of Canford. It was built well inland to keep the population safe from Viking raids. Gradually its importance had been overtaken by the growth of Poole, Bournemouth and Wimborne. Because it did not belong to any of the growth areas, it had no worship building of any other denomination. Those who wished for such went into Wimborne. When the parish began to grow, this turned out to be an important factor, as we welcomed an unusual number of members brought up in Free Churches.

Right on one edge of the parish he also inherited the little mission church at Ashington, a farming hamlet built by the Wimborne estate. This church had been founded in 1900 by Lady Wimborne as a mission to the navvies building the railway that ran next to it. The railway has since gone, but the mission continues, now serving the small local community and those from the rest of the parish who like services according to the 1662 Prayer Book. The Wimborne family were Lords of the Manor of Canford for about a century, becoming famous through the Victorian iron and steel trade. (We still have the first iron bridge in Dorset.) They sat in the pews where a choir would normally sit, which are still called the 'squire stalls'. Lady Wimborne sat next to the Vicar in a special seat twice the width of the others, designed to accommodate her Victorian-style dresses!

During the 1920s the Wimborne estate was sold, and the buildings became a new Public School with a Christian foundation. The school still uses the parish church as its chapel, and is a very positive influence in the parish.

In 1971 Canford Magna was still 'the village', one street dominated by the school, with a developed area towards Wimborne, and ribbon development scattered round the area. All was private housing stretching from a road where planning permission allowed only one house per five acres, to the old estate cottages. The population was perhaps five or six thousand. The congregation was small – about twenty-five in the morning and six in the evening. They had accepted Series 2 services and brought the holy table down to the chancel step, and there was a happy informality about services, which were all led from the front. There was no marked churchmanship. During the week the only activity was a Ladies Guild. This had been formerly a Mothers Union group, and had then optimistically become a Young Wives Group. (There is a picture in their scrap book of the oldest young wife, probably seventy-five, cutting their birthday cake!) There was some link with Scouts and Guides, but otherwise no organisations during the week. There was a small choir.

It was obvious, however, that change was going to come. A start had been made on the new estates of Oakley and Merley, and a site had been accepted for a new church. The developer of this estate was a keen Methodist who had offered the site to the Methodists of Wimborne. They, however, were unable to accept it, as they had just rebuilt their main church. So it was offered to us on condition that we built on it within five years. Poole was becoming the fastest growing borough in the country, and people moving to its new industries were looking for new houses. Our area was one of those scheduled to meet this need.

John Collins

The new Vicar, John Collins, was to preside over ten years of exciting growth. Coming from St Mark's, Gillingham, where they had seen great blessing, he was previously Curate of All Souls, Langham Place, and President of the Christian Union at Cambridge University. It was there that I first came under his influence. He was a gifted preacher and evangelist, with a wife, Diana, also talented in evangelism and drama. Both were people soaked in prayer. He had a clear sense of purpose yet a gentleness of approach. At an early Church Council meeting he is recorded as saying 'I will make changes, but will make haste slowly.' Though never setting himself up as a party man, he brought with him an Evangelical love of the gospel and a charismatic experience. Neither word was used, however.

He came with the promise of a Curate once the parish reached a certain size. He was a man to match the future of the parish rather than its past. As well as receiving a generally kindly welcome, he found as Lay Reader Hugh Morgan Williams – a school governor, Lay Chairman of the

Diocesan Synod, and respected local surgeon, who was prepared to give himself totally to the work of the parish. In those early years the congregation experienced a gradual opening to the light, and warming of spirit, rather than a dramatic change of tack.

Explaining growth

How does one explain the growth of the parish from a Sunday attendance of double figures to roughly 750 at present?

1. *The goodness of the Lord.* We want all the glory to go to the Lord for what has happened and will happen. Indeed we have many signs that, for all the good people we have been given, the credit is all his. We can only worship that he has been so good to us, and humbly ask for more. To keep us from pride, we keep getting people joining us for whom we can claim no credit. One Sunday afternoon a man cycled past the parish church, which is down a side road and can easily be missed. He felt the need to go in, found himself in a baptism sevice, felt the desire to come again, and found the Lord. Another woman living in our parish but never attending church found the Lord on a visit to South Africa. There she joined a live Baptist church. She told the minister that she doubted if such churches existed in England, to find that he had visited our church on her doorstep only a year before. She has been a great joy to us ever since. Another young wife rang up out of the blue, having received our church Christmas card. As the clergyman went through the door she asked, 'How do I become a Christian?' The Lord had prepared her by dreams. Others again are referred by charity groups helping to sort out a crisis.

2. *The power of prayer.* John Collins had founded the growth of the church on prayer, and over the years it has become possible to see that at the centre of every group in the church there was a nucleus of praying leaders. Last year we were able for the first time to report that every area of the church life now had such a group. The Church Council starts its meetings with a half-hour of prayer, and many members come having prayed through the agenda. We believe now

that no one would be likely to be elected (and the competition is stiff) unless they put prayer high on their priorities. A few of our members see prayer as their main ministry in the church, and as a staff we value those who promise to pray for us daily. Some have a special gift of listening to the Lord, and share with us what they sense the Lord is saying. This is then checked by the staff.

At the moment we are being led to see prayer as our special calling, and we are about to have a prayer fortnight before Easter, in which we are calling all our members to listen to God together. Before nearly all services a group will meet to pray for the Lord to touch that event. This prayer is not all asking, but has a large element of praise. In this way we believe the Lord teaches us to think big, because he is big. This has meant, for example, that in our giving we have stopped all money-raising 'efforts', because these teach people to think small. Giving is in response to the Lord's goodness, and our people are taught to start thinking about giving at the level of tithing. So we have been able to build our last new church almost entirely from the giving of our members, and to sustain a budget that this year has risen to £87,000. We find the Lord never gives us much over, and at the moment money is tight, but we have also never had to stop an event purely on money grounds.

3. *The arrival of individuals.* When the Collins family came, as well as using the people already in the church, they prayed for six new couples, free of obvious problems, who could make a nucleus for the new growth. One member of that group, who is still a pastoral leader, had come from a Brethren background, and was finding it hard to find fellowship on a half-built estate. Visited by a church member, he asked 'Is the Vicar keen?' Hearing that he had been a Curate at All Souls, he came! At his first service he and his wife felt the Lord saying 'This is your home now'. They and the other couples went the second mile from then on. Some of these, coming from Free Church backgrounds, had a great love of the Bible, and a long history of teaching. All were confirmed in the end, and have accepted the discipline of the Anglican church loyally. At least one couple are now in the Anglican ministry.

Imported also from outside were some excellent Curates: Brian Nicholson, ex-army-officer, and particularly gifted with young couples; John Mumford, with gifts to start a large youth work and organise big events; and now Martyn Cripps, former solicitor, able to cover a wide field and heading up the evangelistic side of the church. All had a desire to evangelise, and all had wives totally behind them.

4. *The building of the staff.* We have always felt that church leadership should be corporate, and that the clergy should be complemented by lay church leaders. So, around the time the Mumfords came, others were added as well. Wives have from the start been treated as full members of staff in so far as their family commitments allowed, and have been in on all decision-making. Then two Non-Stipendiary Ministers came. Ron Dodgson had been ordained while in community ministry and he and his wife, Jean, came to work by faith in the parish. Roy Wyatt, a surveyor, took the local ordination course, and for several years was on the staff while keeping his job as well. He and his wife have now transferred to the stipendiary ministry and work elsewhere in the diocese. Peter and Ann Scott, former missionaries, also felt called to the parish. Peter kept a part-time teaching job. They both have been pastoral leaders, and Peter also churchwarden.

Later, when the office work increased, an administrator was appointed to run a parish office. All routine work is done through that, leaving the other staff free for spiritual priorities. Later a youth worker, Richard Landall, was appointed – paid, like the administrator, by the congregation. Under John Mumford and Richard the youth work increased greatly. We have, however, had to cut this back somewhat as we had expanded beyond our capacity to produce leadership teams. Having now made this a matter of prayer, we hope to reopen part of the work we closed, with new leaders offering. We feel, though, that we have learnt from this to put quality before quantity. We need to settle how much of our resources should go to youth rather than adult work.

5. *An emphasis on groups.* Though many names have been mentioned, we have tried to avoid too much emphasis on individuals. We are the Body of Christ, and individuals are

converted into it. As numbers have grown this has meant that we could still keep the personal note. To begin with, one group met in the Vicarage for Bible study, then went over to the church, where John donned a cassock and led prayers. In this way people from a more traditional background did not feel threatened. When the overflow had begun to invade the Vicarage bedrooms, this was altered to a system of housegroups, originally three.

As groups began to multiply, the problem of leadership increased. So a system of pastoral leaders was started. There were seven of these, and each led their own group. The title 'elders' was considered but rejected as it did not fit an Anglican ethos, and their job description was pastoral rather than that of decision-making. When I came here, there were twelve groups under eight leaders. This meant that the beginning of a second layer of leadership was started. Some of these original pastoral leaders began to feel that the demands were too high, as they were men capable of holding down a responsible secular job. They also had some feeling that they were not living up to the expectations of the church leadership. Today we have twenty-one groups under seven pastoral leaders. Every group has its own male leader, and we have introduced a level of second leader. Most of these are leaders in training.

We encourage groups to pray that they will get too big, and so have to split. In this way splitting becomes an achievement and not a threat to precious fellowship. The groups meet fortnightly, and the leaders meet with their pastoral leader for prayer regularly. We find it does not work to have pastoral leaders also leading their own group, though they often take the lead when they visit a group. Alongside the mixed group system there is a series of twelve groups for women who do not go out to work. These meet each week in term time. These women's groups arrange their own programmes, with some groups being evangelistic in intent, others with a teaching and support aim. The mixed groups all do the same course each term, and usually get a visit from a clergy member of staff once a term, when we will cover a subject of general interest to the parish. We are just experimenting with a new type of group designed for retired people who cannot keep up with a fairly fast course. These are based on coffee mornings with a more informal Bible study after.

We recognise that any group system runs the danger of being divisive, though so far we have only had one group we were unhappy about. However, to avoid the possibility of division, apart from prayer covering, I meet the pastoral leaders most weeks, usually for breakfast, so we keep open communications. They do the same with their group leaders. We also meet fortnightly at the Lantern, one of our dual-purpose buildings. The majority of the group members attend this, so that Tuesday night becomes parish night. I see the Lantern group, at the moment with about 160 attending, as the nucleus of the spiritual life of the parish, where all moves forward will start. Usually at the Lantern we divide into four or five teaching groups for the first half of the evening, and then come together for praise and prayer in the second half.

I acknowledge that this programme puts a lot of pressure on our senior laymen, and am glad that they are willing to do it cheerfully. However, we do appoint people to posts for three years, with a chance to change after that. In this way they keep fresh. Sometimes we change them faster. One very good pastoral leader had to resign because he was promoted to a very demanding secular job. Others resigned because they became too tired. We have thought a lot recently about this, and feel that perhaps some were pushed into jobs they were not ready for, and we try to train people more now. All round, though, the cheerfulness of these men warms the heart.

6. *Outside links.* We have often found that visiting speakers have been the best people to introduce new ideas. In the early days members of the Post Green Community helped by their presence and joy in worship. In more recent years parish weekends have been growth points, led by such people as Michael Whinney, Tom Walker, Michael Harper and Jackie Pullinger.

Though attenders from outside have always been welcomed, we have aimed to be a church for Canford Parish. If people did come from outside, they were encouraged to commit themselves totally, and if possible move into the parish area. Sermon tasters have been discouraged. The proportion of the Electoral Roll from outside the parish has varied between twenty and twenty-seven per cent.

7. *The use of spiritual gifts.* We believe, as did St Paul in 1 Corinthians 12, that all Christians are given something to contribute to the Body of Christ, and so we have encouraged musical gifts, counselling, healing, drama, dance, etc. Groups exercising such gifts tend to alter with their membership, and sometimes take a rest, but basically we want those who have a certain gift, well-developed or embryonic, to get together and prayerfully practise that gift for joint use in the church. In some of our services we value the use of the gift of prophecy, or the linked gifts of tongues with interpretation. These need checking against Scripture.

Musically the small choir soon died a natural death, and we did not resurrect it. In its place we have three worship groups, an orchestra, and individual singers who are co-ordinated by the Worship Committee. Most services now have a group leading worship before the formal service starts. This helps to get a good start, and to cut down the chatter of all friendly churches! Dance and drama groups usually meet regularly to pray and seek guidance. Then when something is ready, it is offered to the staff and used. More recently our musical director has written a Christian musical which has been performed for two seasons in one of our churches and in the Bournemouth Playhouse. Such a mammoth effort, using about a hundred people, has put some strain on the normal activities but has, we believe, given us a new vision of what the Lord can release from our ordinary members.

As many of our members come from totally non-church backgrounds, we find that much needs to be put right in their lives under the influence of the Holy Spirit. Thus over the years a counselling ministry has developed which is now taking a more organised form under Jean Dodgson, with about thirty members involved. Prayer for healing takes place regularly in the groups, and also in our monthly evening Communion service. Occasionally we have a whole service given over to healing prayer, teaching and testimonies.

8. *Building new centres.* We have been fortunate in being able to build two new dual-purpose buildings on our new estates in a period of six years. In 1976 the Lantern was built on the site given by the developer. This was seen originally as a community centre, though with most of the activities led by our members. At first we held only a monthly family service, which has just this year become weekly. There has been some ill-feeling in the area that we kept most activities under our own control even to the extent of running a closed Sunday School, so that parents had also to be church attenders. Practice has shown that this has brought parents to the Lord, instead of taking responsibility away from them.

The Bearwood centre was opened in 1982. This area is separated from the rest of the parish by a mile of green belt. Originally it had few houses, but a change of the road structure meant that we were given an area of bungalows and council estate. At the same time the rest of the area began to develop. This is now our biggest area and is still growing. It was exciting to have a keen Christian architect and builder, so that prayer went on throughout the building programme, and the church was opened debt-free with about £100,000 raised by the congregation, mostly in two gift days. At an earlier stage this level of giving would have been impossible, and we were blessed by a very substantial permanent loan to help us build the Lantern. Though we had no choice about where to build the Bearwood centre, the final maps show it to be central to the whole estate. The best town planners are in Heaven!

As a short-term result of starting new centres, the numbers at the parish church have dropped. As it was uncomfortably full before, the empty seats challenge us to further growth.

In the build-up of our new centres, the groups have played an important part. The Lantern covers basically the same estate as the parish church, and the two have always been run together. Bearwood is separate, but we were able to start six groups in the area before the church was opened. This meant that the church started with a nucleus of about ninety members. One exciting move has been that three church families have built their new homes on adjacent sites on the newest estate, thus forming a mini-community.

9. *Fostering of community links.* Both the Lantern and Bearwood buildings were opened before any secular community centre. So both centres seek to meet the needs of the community, where these have a Christian antidote. We do not believe, for instance, that we exist 'to keep youth off the streets'. However, there is a lot of loneliness on new estates, so both centres run mothers and toddlers groups, where often lonely mums are recommended to go by the social workers. A few Christian mothers are there too, who seek to befriend and to share Christ as the perfect friend. There is so much noise from children that personal conversations do not embarrass. For older children both centres have playgroups, which meet a need for the child, and again provide one way to befriend mums. Those who express interest are then taken to a Thursday morning enquirer's group, where they often find the Lord. We do not find door-to-door visiting very profitable, but this meeting of felt needs is. One mother whose boy was in a playgroup was nearly killed in a car crash. After months in hospital with occasional clergy visits it was the playgroup leader who befriended her, took her to a Thursday group, brought her to a Guest Service where she committed her life to the Lord, and helped her develop her faith. This autumn she will, we hope, take over the leadership of one of the playgroups. A similar need is met by the fortnightly lunch club for pensioners at the Lantern. Working more slowly, they try to share the love of a Saviour to whom it is never too late to turn.

10. *Evangelism.* We have never had a parish mission, though we are at the moment considering a faith-sharing visit to us. Our main method of evangelism has been to seek to make the fellowship of the Body of Christ so attractive that those who come to us stay, and in due course find the reason. Most of those who respond to the preaching at a Guest Service are at the end of a process of being drawn in. Although our members played a large part in a Festival led by David Watson in Poole, the results locally were disappointing. Similarly two diocesan events in which we played a loyal part do not seem to have produced lasting results. The more successful of these was a youth mission in

Wimborne known as 'Down to Earth', which came just at the right time for reaping a harvest in our youth work. We feel convinced that we are meant to be a 'honeypot' church rather than one broadcasting gospel darts into the community. The danger of this is that some of our members can just enjoy the relationship without seeking to attract others in.

11. *Our leadership pattern.* We feel led to an increasingly shared leadership which has an accepted discipline so that we do not have individuals doing their own thing. We ask each leader to accept the discipline of a group, and this includes myself. Having however agreed on a policy which we feel the Lord has confirmed, we then ask for vigorous leadership and give full backing from the centre. We believe also in recognising and encouraging gifts, and our last Christmas thank-you letter to leaders went out to over 200 people. When I came, I sensed that there was too big a gap between leaders and led, so we have tried to close this by making intermediate levels of leaders, thus trying to stop professionalism. Our big word is 'encouragement', and if we had a patron saint it would be Barnabas. We pray for a sense of humour, a willingness to make mistakes, and a readiness to forgive. Most of our leadership training is now by the apprenticeship method.

Perhaps mention should be made of the way the four churches are led. The three clergy circulate, though with a slight preference to leading worship at the church nearest to which we live. We have recently appointed deputy wardens at the church centres who are the link men, rather than clergy. The parish church also has deputy wardens to leave the main wardens free to oversee each area. We recognise that we can push our laity too hard.

At the centre of all this are the staff, who become the spiritual think-tank of the parish. At one time we seemed to have an effective power of veto. In theory we still have this, but try to use it to bend rather than block. Mainly we see ourselves as a group who are privileged to spend more time than most praying together, and seek to serve the parish by our prayers. Increasingly important, and occasionally painful, are our staff quiet days. The Church Council make all policy decisions, but do not greatly influence the execution of that policy. They also fulfil a valuable role as the eyes and ears of the church. Often they will start an issue with a short discussion, to give the likely feel of the congregation. This is then discussed in depth by the staff or an ad hoc committee, who will bring back a paper of suggested action to the P.C.C. which usually, though not always, accepts it. We would rather postpone a decision than push one through when there has not been time to pray it over.

12. *Have we suffered division in the church?* Though we have never had dramatically sudden changes, over the years most things have changed and will probably continue to do so. A few people have left over such issues as the introduction of 'The Peace', or the change of services. However, we have a churchmanship which is not extreme, and we find that the charismatic element which is quietly there tends to cover over the more normal divisions of Catholic and Evangelical. Perhaps more pressure comes as the presence of the Holy Spirit challenges us all to greater holiness. The God-given love enables most people to accept this, but some tend to move to the sidelines, at least for a while. Fortunately we have good links with our neighbouring churches, and people happily move both ways over our boundaries.

The present and the future

We hope that change is now built into our system, not for its own sake but in response to a God who is on the move. I remember a Bishop once saying that 'change is the angel of an unchanging God.' Thus we find our services change in flavour. Some time ago we were led to change from Family Services aimed largely at children to a balance of Family Communion and a more adult-orientated family service. The family we serve is not the nuclear family with young children, but the family of God of all ages. More recently we have felt convicted about the wordiness of our services, and are beginning to get to grips with silence as a way by which we hear the Lord. At our Lantern mid-week meetings we are, for a while, moving away from separate teaching groups

and keeping the whole church together. Here also we are
learning the value of a simple unstructured Eucharist with
no sense of rush. In this we follow the new American Prayer
Book, which has an order of Communion with no set words
but an order of events. This gives us the balance between
freedom and order.

We are fortunate in that all our buildings are small,
seating between two and three hundred. This means that
however large the congregation gets, no one service can be
impersonal. Instead we have had to double the number of
morning services in the last three years. This has meant a
reversal of previous policy which put great emphasis on the
unity of the parish. Now we let the individual churches have
more sense of their own identity, but give prominence to a
few central activities. At the moment these are the Tuesday
evenings at the Lantern, and the Sunday evening service.
Perhaps most important are the Sundays when, three times a
year, we close down all morning services and move into the
Assembly Hall of Canford School, kindly lent to us. Here we
can seat over six hundred, and they are great occasions.
Perhaps the most memorable one was when two recently-
converted adults who had never been baptized asked for
baptism by immersion. So the whole congregation went from
the Assembly Hall to the bank of the River Stour that runs
by, where the Vicar and Curate, wearing wet-suits, baptized
them. A very unliturgical round of applause greeted them as
they came out of the water, and photographs show what a
deep spiritual experience it was!

Specific Prayer. In recent years we feel we have been taught to
pray for specific targets, and that the text 'You have not
because you ask not' applies to vague general prayers. It is to
God's glory that the answers to specific prayers can be
recorded. We feel we have a long way to go in this, and have
some disappointment that the prayer triplet scheme of
Mission England has not particularly caught on. Where it
has done so, however, we have already seen some lovely
answers.

Our biggest challenge has been when we felt the Lord
calling us to set a target for growth. This came about through
a visit by Eddie Gibbs (a former Curate of mine who knows

my weaknesses as a Vicar!). He came to spend a morning with the staff. Of his many wise remarks, one we could not forget was a statement that a parish doing normal things well should get ten per cent of its population in church. It was with some shock that we realised that for a parish of 15,000 we were only recording about three and a half per cent. So before Eddie came back to attend the Church Council we wrote a paper setting a target of 1,500 attenders, not just in church but growing and maturing in Christ. Needless to say, this target gave the staff and P.C.C. considerable misgivings, especially as we felt it right to put a four-year time scale against it. However, the P.C.C. agreed it *nem. con.* and it has remained our main prayer target ever since. At the time of writing we are still behind schedule, and the temptation was to keep quiet about this figure, so we ask your prayers that the results may glorify a God who cannot fail. The recent months have been a time of some sorting out in the congregation, and we believe the Lord is ensuring that all the glory for the results comes to him.

So the story will go on. We marvel at the Lord's goodness and grace. Especially we give thanks for being in the parish at a time of his activity. We have a growing sense of excitement at his future work, and an increased amazement that he wants to involve us in it. In telling this story names have had to be mentioned, but we look forward to the time when in the Body of Christ only one name matters. In the words of a song we often sing:

Father we love you,
we worship and adore you,·
glorify YOUR NAME in all the earth.

Appendix

Contributing ministers were asked to cover the following points in their assessment of their church's growth.

1. Description of position of church – local community, mix of population, building, past history of the church prior to growth. Particular areas of sensitivity within congregation or amongst local community. Local problems and needs. Is the population in area increasing and if so, where from and why?

2. Pattern of church attendance and giving over past 10 years or so. What would a typical Sunday morning service have been like 10 years ago?

3. What started the growth? Were there false starts, problems, risks, resentments? Did you start with a theory or with a pragmatic approach? Did you begin with small groups or a particular evangelistic programme? What part did prayer and Bible study play, or a midweek church meeting, for example? Did you try and emphasise the need for evangelism in all aspects of the church's life?

4. What changes were observable in music and worship? In giving?

5. What part did the various organisations, such as Sunday School, young people, young wives, men's and women's fellowships, etc., play?

6. What do you feel has been attracting new people to come to the church? Are most of them new converts, or lapsed Christians, or from other less lively churches? (Give figures and actual examples if possible: the more 'human' the better). How were new people contacted? Are those who have responded representative of the social spread of the community?

7. How were newcomers brought to the point of decision and commitment?

8. How were they followed up and incorporated into the life of the church? What have new converts contributed to church life?

9. How has your reputation for growth affected your relationship with other churches in the area?

10. What has been the impact on the local community as a whole? Are you offering any new services, such as crèche, care for elderly, opportunities for the unemployed, more youth activities?

11. How, if at all, has the church's relationship with missionaries/missionary societies changed over the past few years?

12. How has the senior leadership of the church changed? Have elders been appointed, for instance? Was some relinquishing of your own power or centrality a necessary step forward? Have you felt pressure from church members to be a traditional, more authoritative figure? To what extent do you think the growth of the church is a result of your own presence there?

13. What administrative arrangements have been made to allow the church to grow? What changes do you now envisage to stimulate and sustain further growth?

14. What have been the potential areas of personal hurt in the growth process? Have you been able to avoid them, or found it necessary to tackle them vigorously? As minister do you feel that your own authority has been attacked? Do you feel that the leadership of the church generally is more

flexible? Humble? Willing to share leadership roles? Open to new ideas?

15. Looking back, what would you have done differently? Looking forward, what do you feel is coming next?

Also from MARC Europe

MICHAEL GRIFFITHS
(Editor)

Ten Sending Churches

Ten ministers from different areas and different denominations describe how their church has become actively involved in mission.

Mission is a sadly neglected field today. Too many churches are too consumed with their own problems to appreciate the link between mission, evangelism and a living and growing Christian fellowship. What is needed is a series of models: churches which have seen the importance of mission and have responded to the need for committed and prayerful support.

There is no single 'right' way of backing mission. Here, however, are imaginative approaches which will provide real examples of how your church can participate in the spreading of the Gospel.

Michael Griffiths is Principal of London Bible College and Consulting Director of the Overseas Missionary Fellowship.

Published jointly with the Evangelical Missionary Alliance and S.T.L. Books.

PETER BRIERLEY (Editor)

UK Christian Handbook
1985/86 Edition

Foreword by Lord Donald Coggan

The *UK Christian Handbook* is the only complete, comprehensive
reference book on Christian life in the UK: an essential resource for
ministers, managers and administrators. It lists virtually all
Christian organisations in the UK. For this new edition every single
entry has been updated and hundreds added. For ease of reference
it has been carefully and thoroughly reorganised after a wide survey
of customers' needs.

Do you want a phone number? An address? The name of a chief
executive? Turnover? The aims, publications or staff of a given
group? *Look it up here.*

- Bookshops
- Missionary Societies
- Youth Organisations
- Denominational Headquarters
- Children's Homes
- Retreat and Conference Centres
- Relief Agencies

- Adoption Agencies
- Theological Colleges
- Publishers
- Art and Layout Services
- Video Producers
- Tour Operators
- *and many more*

User aids include a variety of maps and contents indexed by person,
location and organisation.

'I have been surprised and delighted, in leafing through the *UK
Christian Handbook*, to see the wealth of information which it
contains.'   *Lord Donald Coggan*

'This is a most amazing document . . . an indispensable fount of
information.'   *Michael Green*

'A mine of information . . . I commend the total publication
wholeheartedly.'   *Donald English*

'You can survive in Christian work without the *UK Christian
Handbook* – but you'll always be borrowing somebody else's.'
                                                    Gilbert W. Kirby

Published jointly with the Evangelical Alliance and Bible Society.